Sounding The Drum

Community Building in the Digital Age

Lori Gosselin

Copyright © 2017 Lori Gosselin
ISBN: 978-0-9876840-4-2
All rights reserved.

For my most precious community;
Team Gosselin

CONTENTS

1

It's Time

Something is stirring. Can you feel it? A quiet, steady movement is underway. The world is marching toward community.

In 1987, M. Scott Peck M.D. published *The Different Drum: Community Making and Peace*, an important work that offered a comprehensive definition of "community". Yet, all these years later, there are few more overused or misunderstood words in the English language.

We yearn for community because it represents to us a feeling of belonging. We seek connection with others because we are social beings. But community is more than just a feeling of belonging or togetherness. Community is more than a group of individuals with shared values, goals, interests, and beliefs; more than people who work, party or worship together. Community is hope for the human race: This is a movement of hope.

Community will lead us to the discovery of the answers we desperately need personally-- and globally. It is only in genuine community that we experience the truth of this statement: *We are all in this together.*
In community we find the greatest joys life has to offer. In community, we discover the true power to change the world.

Listen. Can you hear the beat of the drums?

2

The Spirit of Community

"The gem of community is so exquisitely beautiful
it may seem unreal to you,
like a dream you once had
when you were a child..."
~M. Scott Peck, M.D.
The Different Drum: Community Making and Peace

Community saved my life. It was the people huddled around me after my twenty-three-year-old son Alex died that helped me to survive the unthinkably-dark months that followed. Community supported me at other times in my life too; times when I was lonely, times when I felt lost, times when I needed an anchor in turbulent seas.

I have long loved the feeling of being in a group of people who care about one another. During every significant chapter of my life, I have found myself in the midst of such a group. Each of those groups was like the friend who comes along at just the right time and stays until the purpose of the friendship has been achieved. When I was thirty, I read Peck's *The Different Drum* and recognized that in those groups, I had experienced different aspects of community. In pouring over Peck's work, I began to understand what community really is. But my story begins long before I heard of M. Scott Peck, back when I thought "community" was just an ordinary word.

This is my story.

The Cross Country Team

I was sixteen years old and just starting grade eleven when two of my friends announced that they were joining the school's Cross Country running team and they wanted me to join too. I don't know why they invited me or why I accepted. Katherine and Laura were athletic; I was not. It was a struggle for me to complete the first two-mile run; more jogging than running, and this was just the warm-up. I'm glad I did join the team, though. It was to be a wonderful experience of the support and camaraderie of a community.

I credit our coach for this. Mr. Edwards emphasized the fact that we were a team, and this was important. Thanks to his leadership, we had something that many of the other teams didn't: We had team spirit. We were not a strong team - our runners didn't win or place often - but that didn't matter because winning was not our only goal.

On the weekends, we traveled to compete with other schools in Cross Country meets. The courses for the meets, three to four miles long, snaked through the woods. During the races, we might splash through brooks, scale cliffs, stumble over tree roots, climb hills and slog down muddy roads. As the organizers walked us over the course to familiarize us with the route, we would talk about how we would negotiate the more challenging parts of the course, mentally preparing together for the race.

When it was time for the boys to race, the girls spread out over the course to cheer for them. We positioned ourselves at the top of a cliff or beside a brook, or along the home stretch. The boys did the same for us. When I was getting low on energy, and I came upon my teammates cheering for me, I somehow found the strength to keep going.

After the meet, we returned to the van sweaty and spent, and discussed our runs on the drive home. We laughed, complained and empathized with one another. I was always at peace with my performance no matter how well or badly I did. For me, being a part of the team trumped everything.

At sixteen, I knew that something special was at play. I know, now, that my experience on the Cross Country team was a microcosm for the best part of life; community. Even though you performed better in some races than in others, your team supported you unconditionally. As you ran your race and grew tired, the presence and encouragement of your teammates sustained you. Even when your teammates were far ahead or behind you, you never felt alone.

I adored being on this team! I was a part of something special; welcomed, supported, and accepted, just because I was there.

Book Club

My husband and I were operating our small business and raising our two young children when I read Scott Peck's first book, *The Road Less Traveled: A New Psychology of Love, Traditional Values and Spiritual Growth.* I loved the book and thought it would be fun to make it the subject of a Book Club so I would have the opportunity to explore it thoroughly. Responding to my invitations, a dozen women read the book and then gathered in my living room to discuss the idea of forming a Book Club. We decided that we would meet once a month.

I knew a Book Club would provide a social outing for me, but by the time we met for the first time to discuss the book, I had just finished reading *The Different Drum, and* I knew the Book Club might also be an opportunity to be a part of a group that was evolving into a community.

At our first meeting, we opened our books and read the first sentence, *"Life is difficult."* We paused there, each of us resonating with that statement. We began to talk about it, one by one tentatively sharing the struggles we faced as parents, as women--as human beings. I listened in astonishment: These women were intelligent, poised and established in their careers, yet they too harboured fears and insecurities. In their company, I felt supported and less alone.

Book Club became a safe place for me to share my problems, knowing they would be met with support, acceptance and understanding. This monthly gathering of kindred souls had come at just the right time in my life, yet it wasn't the last time I would find a community just when I needed it.

Neighbourhoods

In 1986, my husband and I moved from our apartment in Moncton across the river and into our first house in the town of Riverview. The front door faced Coverdale Road, the main road of the town, making it a perfect location for our small business. The back door, driveway, and yard faced Wilmot Avenue, a residential street where several young families lived.

As we moved our things into our new house, I recalled the day my parents and three siblings and I moved into our house in Moncton when I was eight years old. My sister and I were riding our bikes on the street in front of the house in this strange new neighbourhood when I saw a woman walking up the driveway carrying sandwiches, lemonade, and a thermos of coffee. This welcoming gesture marked the beginning of a long kinship that my mother would enjoy with the other women in the neighbourhood. Remembering this, I was excited: Now I would have a neighbourhood of my own!

But times were different in 1986 than they were in 1967. Many of the women on Wilmot worked and were not free to socialize as my mother and her neighbours had been. Though I longed for the

camaraderie that my mother had experienced with her neighbours, most of my interactions were with customers who came to the front (business) door, rang the doorbell and waited; few were with neighbours who tapped on the back door window and let themselves in.

Although the children on Wilmot played together, the relationships among the parents were sporadic. We waved to one another while raking leaves, working in our gardens or shovelling our driveways. We saw one another at meet-the-teacher night, at the voting station at election time, or on Halloween nights when the kids were still too young to trick-or-treat alone. We didn't grow close to our neighbours, yet there was an invisible web that connected us that I didn't recognize until the very end.

After living on Coverdale Road for twenty years, when our daughter was in her first year of university and our son was in Grade eleven, we purchased a house on eleven acres on a country road outside of Riverview. We continued to live on Coverdale Road for several more months while we renovated the house in the country.

As I prepared for the move, I thought about how much the neighbourhood had changed in twenty years. Most of the original neighbours had moved away, and Ruth, a good friend who had lived on the other corner of Wilmot and Coverdale, had died three years earlier. Still, I felt sad to think of leaving the place where our children were born and had spent their childhoods.

Then I learned that Joy, a neighbour who lived two doors up on Wilmot, was moving away too. It occurred to me that she was the only one left to say goodbye to. One afternoon, I looked out my kitchen window and saw her weeding her flowerbed. I decided to go up the street to say goodbye.

We stood next to her flowerbed discussing her upcoming move and mine, both admitting how strange it felt to think of leaving the neighbourhood. We were poignantly aware that we were about to abandon the setting of a precious phase of our lives.

Finally, when we had said all there was to say and silence descended on us, Joy and I hugged. It was a gesture that said more than our words could have possibly said. We had never hugged before.

That hug stays with me to this day. It made me wonder, and I wonder still, how it is possible that we miss significant connections in our environment. We are so much more important to one another than we realize.

The Farmer's Market

We had been living in the country for two years, and as a city girl, I was still adjusting to country living. For twenty years, I had lived in a town where I could look out my kitchen window and see neighbours preparing their suppers as I made mine, or wave to neighbours as they drove home at the end of the day. Though I loved our new property and home, I felt disconnected and isolated in the country.

One autumn day, I made some bracelets by stringing semi-precious gemstones on elastic cords. I gave them as Christmas gifts to my daughter, sisters, and nieces. Everyone loved the bracelets and suggested I sell them at the Saturday morning Farmer's Market in town. Initially, I rejected the idea. There were many talented artists at the Farmer's Market; I was sure I would feel out-of-place there.

I was so wrong. When eventually I decided to give it a try, I found

the diverse population of vendors who sold their wares at the Market warmly welcomed me. I also found a spirit of community there. I had stepped out of my comfort zone and been granted entrance into a magical world.

For the next eighteen months, every Saturday morning I rose at six am, hastily dressed then threw my lunch into a cooler bag while boiling a kettle to make coffee, then I drove the twenty minutes to town. Balancing the weight of my green plastic crate filled with my bracelets, I made my way into the Market. I arranged my jewelry on the table as all around me my neighbours were setting up their booths. When I finished, with thermos in hand, I'd wander through the market to visit the other vendors and catch up on the events of the week.

It was the last Saturday before the holidays on my first Christmas at the Market. The energy was palpably high and the mood festive. Christmas gifts were quietly, spontaneously passed from one vendor to another. I recognized a familiar spirit here, the feeling that these were "my people", that we celebrated one another, that I belonged.

When it came time for me to leave the Market for good, I grieved the loss of my Market community with an intensity that did not surprise me. Because by then, I knew how important it was for me to be a part of a group of people who cared about one another. Mournfully, I wondered where I would find my next community.

I was surprised to find my answer in a most unexpected place because by now the child of the digital age, technology, had produced a child of her own and she had come of age: Social media would enable my next group experience which would happen online.

3

Digitally- Enabled Communities

"Both the history of the telephone
and the early evidence on the Internet usage
strongly suggest that computer-mediated communication
will turn out to complement, not replace,
face-to-face communities."
~Robert D. Putnam
Bowling Alone: The Collapse and Revival of American Community

The Hangout Group

It was August of 2011. I had been blogging for a year at lifeforinstance.com, a place where we engaged in deep and lively discussions about life's challenging issues, when I learned about Google+ Hangouts. Hangouts were free, live video chats; a platform where up to ten people could have a conversation together online. I was excited; this could be a way to take the conversation off the blog into a more dynamic setting for discussion.

Maybe we could build a community there!

In preparation for the Hangouts, I composed a list of questions with a life theme. I used these questions to guide the discussion. During our video gatherings, we could delve deeply into the topics and have fascinating conversations about life.

In the first two years, a dozen or so people came to the Hangouts, logging in from seven different countries. Some returned several times then drifted away while others remained. Gradually, we settled into a core group of seven people.

Frequently on the Hangouts, I talked about Peck's concept of community. I urged everyone to read *The Different Drum*. Once, I tried to start an online book group to discuss it, but I was unable to get it off the ground.

It was early in December of 2013 when something shifted. We were discussing our wishes for the holidays and for the coming year, when Corinne, rather than answering the question herself, turned to Don to offer her wish *for him.* She said she wished he would find a swift and perfect resolution to the issues he faced. The gesture showed that she had been paying attention, and that she cared. It became quiet on the Hangout as everyone turned his or her attention to Don. He, too, was quiet. He appeared to be touched by her concern.

Inspired by Corinne's action, I suggested that each of us offer our wishes to one another. Everyone liked the idea so we did, one by one bestowing them on one another as gifts.

When we finished, something magical happened. Spontaneously, one by one, everyone began to share how he or she felt about the Hangouts. They said they felt safe here. They expressed astonishment that everyone on the Hangout felt so familiar to them even though no two people in the group had ever met in person. Corinne said she felt like this was her support group, echoing something I'd heard years before at my Book Club.

Later that evening, when I told my daughter Natasha what had happened at the Hangout, she asked: *"Do you have copies of the questions you used to spark discussion?"* I said I did. When our phone call finished, I resumed my research for what I believed would be my next book. An hour and a half had passed before the thought occurred to me:

I should write a book about community building.

Full Disclosure and an Announcement

It was a few months before I had time to start writing, but when I did the words flowed. As I prepared for the next Hangout, I knew I had to tell the group I was writing a book about community building and that the Hangout Group would be an important part of the book and, if they were willing, the subject of an ongoing experiment in community building. Without hesitation, they each offered their consent, encouragement, and support.

This was only the beginning of the story for the Hangout Group. I will pick up the story again in Chapter 5 when I talk about the community building process. But before I even began to write Chapter 5, something intriguing began to happen. One after the other, two offline communities spontaneously sprang to life, both facilitated by technology.

The Keepers of Rte 114

In 2014, a deep snowy winter was followed by a long, cold spring. By late April, there were still large, sand-encrusted piles of snow banking the roads and highways. Spring was beginning to feel like a pipe dream. Then, suddenly, the temperature spiked and held for several days. The snow melted--fast! It flooded waterways and washed away bridges in many small communities in the province.

The small brook on our property swelled to proportions I'd never seen before, overrunning its banks on both sides and spilling onto the patio. I soon learned we had an even bigger problem. The increased water flow had overrun a culvert on the road to town causing erosion that resulted in a twenty-four-foot hole that spanned one lane and spread into the centre of the road rendering it impassable.

My husband went to assess the situation. There he found many of our neighbours staring in disbelief at what they were calling "the sinkhole". They discussed the inconvenience of getting to town via the alternate route, one nearly three times longer, on a narrow, and not so safe, country back-road.

My husband was determined to find a better option since, because of our business, trips to the Post Office in town were a near-daily occurrence for us. So, he got busy and soon returned with a plan.

We drove both of our cars to our side of the sinkhole and parked one car on a side road. Then, in the second car, we travelled the back-road to town and circled back, parking the car on the driveway of a farmer on the other side of the sinkhole. Finally, we walked across the road on the edge of the sinkhole to the first car and drove it back home. Now we had a car positioned on either side of the sinkhole, and by using both vehicles, we could manage our trips to town.

The car juggling was a cumbersome solution but it was a solution that would work for us until they fixed the road.

But then I thought about the inconvenience of carrying our groceries from one car to another, and I ruminated about the upcoming family wedding (walking on the side of the road and up the farmer's long driveway -- in heels). I phoned our neighbour Sammie to complain about the mess. She commiserated with me, saying it was unacceptable that we had heard nothing from our local politician since the road had washed out. We had no idea when the road would be repaired. Rumours suggested it might remain like this until the summer or perhaps until Christmas! Sammie pointed out that there were places in the province where people were facing worse situations than ours; some where the residents had been completely cut off from the nearest town. At least, she said, we *could* get to town.

Then she told me that the washed-out road was proving to be a serious problem for the young couple that owned the fuelling station on this side of the sinkhole. Their business was already down by 93%. Sammie said that John, the owner, had drawn up a petition calling for immediate action. He had the petition on the counter at the store.

I told my husband about the petition. I suggested we invite Sammie and her husband Ken to come over that evening so we could talk about what was happening and see what we could do about it. Then we drove down to the fuelling station to sign the petition and to invite John and his wife to come to the meeting too.

That evening, John, Sammie and Ken came. By the time we had drained our teacups, we had a plan to hold a rally to garner media attention. We also decided to create a Facebook Group for two purposes: to put pressure on politicians, and to keep everyone along Rte. 114 informed. We scheduled another meeting for the following evening.

The next evening, we created the Facebook Group calling it "Keepers of Rte. 114". We invited Facebook friends who lived along the 79-kilometer stretch of road that comprised Rte. 114 to spread the word to other people who were affected by the sinkhole. We formed a tentative plan to have a pre-rally on Friday evening and a larger rally on Sunday afternoon.

But we didn't have to put our rally plans into action. The next morning, Sammie was able to reach the assistant of the politician in our area and he informed her that road engineers were on their way to the sinkhole to see what could be done.

Within a week, there was a Bailey bridge in place that opened one lane on the highway.
By then, the Facebook group had over 200 members. A few days after the road was reopened, something unexpected occurred. When

an accident on Rte. 114 blocked both lanes, a member of Keepers of Rte. 114 posted about it on the Facebook group to alert people who might be planning to go to town. We began to look to the group for information about the accident.

In the months that followed, as we descended into a stormy winter that often made driving precarious, members of the Keepers group posted accident reports, school bus delay notices and road conditions. Before I left for town, I'd post on the page to ask if anybody had been out on the roads and what they were like, and I would often have a response very quickly.

Keepers of Rte. 114 is still evolving. It went from being a place where we could connect to the politicians and keep everyone up to date on what was happening during the episode of the sinkhole, to a place where the people who lived on the 114 can communicate about anything that affects them. The Facebook group continues to increase in size. As I write, nearly three years later, the group is approaching 1400 members.

The sinkhole episode altered my experience of living in the country. Before it happened, I felt isolated and disconnected, but now I felt a sense of unity with the families spread out along this country road.

Moncton Strong

One evening two months after the sinkhole incident, I was watching television with my husband when I received an email from a friend who lived out of town. *"Are you guys okay?"* she wrote, *"I heard about the shootings in Moncton!"*

I opened my laptop and went to Facebook, to the Keeper's group, knowing I'd find news there. I learned that earlier that day, a young man had shot and killed three young RCMP officers in Moncton and had injured two others. The police were searching for the shooter and were advising the general public to stay inside and to lock their doors.

We heard rumours that he had friends in our area, so we, too, locked our doors. The Internet became our window on the situation. Everywhere, people were glued to the news, but not the television news--the more immediate social media postings on Facebook and Twitter. A Twitter hashtag sprang up, #PrayForMoncton.

For two days and two nights, the shooter was at large. On the second night, prompted by a request spread by social media, the people of Moncton and surrounding areas left their porch lights on to assist the police in finding him. It was late that night when he was finally taken into custody.

Now #PrayForMoncton became #MonctonMourns and #MonctonStrong as we turned our attention to the grieving process. On the steps of the RCMP building, flowers, gifts, candles, and cards appeared and spilled out onto the sidewalk. Businesses changed their roadside signs to read, "Thank you RCMP / MonctonStrong."

As city officials began to make preparations for the funeral services, they realized the Moncton Coliseum, our largest venue, would not be able to accommodate the number of people expected to attend, so they made arrangements for eleven large buildings to live-stream the funeral services on video screens. The casino, the university, and several churches and theatres prepared places for us to mourn together.

On the day of the funeral services, the people of Greater Moncton wore red, the color of the RCMP uniform. As they watched the services on the large screens in those venues, the people rose when the members of the congregation in the Coliseum were asked to stand, and they sat when the people in the Coliseum sat. The national news anchor who was covering the funerals said, *"Today we are all from Moncton."*

Throughout the crisis and during the aftermath, people showed their support on social media with updates and photos. We wrote that we couldn't sleep, that we were worried and sad -- and we reached out to comfort one another. When the funeral services were over, and the rain stopped that afternoon, people posted photos of the rainbow they saw over the city of Moncton.

Within the space of days, we came to know something that people of a community know intimately; we are all in this together.

Social media-enabling technology has radically changed our experience of civic tragedy. In the past, communication was one-way; from television to us but technology has made our communication responsive and interactive; the true genesis of community building.

4

What is a Community?

*"We were born to unite with our fellow men
and to join in community
with the human race."*
~Cicero

In 1987, Scott Peck wrote that there was much confusion about the meaning of the word community. Since then, this confusion has only increased. Today, we use the word to refer to every type of group from clubs, societies, social media followings and organizations, to the citizens of cities, towns and countries. "Community" has become interchangeable with "group".

A true community is something with a spirit at its essence. Not every building with bedrooms, kitchen, bathrooms and a family room is a home; nor is every group of people who live, work, worship or socialize together a community. Much like calling every house a home, this application of the word community is an assumption about a group based on how it looks *from the outside.*

So, what then, is a community? It is a unique set of committed relationships among an inclusive group of people who communicate authentically, who celebrate together, and who care about, respect, and support one another. A community is a group of people who are aware of the truth and importance of this statement, *"we are all in this together."*

Have you ever been in a place where you were celebrated *for exactly who you are*, where you knew you belonged and you were highly valued by everyone around you? Can you claim as your own a place where you feel supported, where you enjoy camaraderie and meaningful conversation, yet you are as comfortable as if you were in your home wearing pyjamas with your feet up and a mug of hot cocoa in your hands?

Have you ever been a part of a group where you were accepted and loved *just because you were there?*

The Seven Pillars of Community

Seven characteristics give a group the distinction of being called a community. Like pillars towering over ancient landscapes, these characteristics define a space where a community can grow.

- **Commitment**
- **Inclusivity**
- **Shared Leadership**
- **Collaboration**
- **Camaraderie**
- **Authenticity**
- **Support**

The seven pillars are interdependent. For instance, the commitment of the members facilitates a willingness to be authentic which makes a community a supportive place. The shared leadership and inclusivity enable the members to be collaborative.

Each pillar is essential; the absence of even one is an indication that you're not talking about a community; you're talking about a group. (The group may be on the path to community, however. More about this in Chapter 5.)

Commitment

"Commitment is what transforms
a promise
into a reality."
~Abraham Lincoln

Building community takes time, dedication and patience. A group evolves into community as the relationships among the members grow. Commitment is a crucial factor in this growth process, just as it is an integral component in developing any relationship. We find it easier to trust one another when we know we are all committed to the outcome of building community.

The commitment of the members creates an environment for inclusivity, authenticity, the ability to use consensus and the feeling of camaraderie and support. Commitment is where community building begins, and when it persists, it can take the group all the way to the end of the process.

A lack of commitment on the part of even one member can be detrimental to the community building process, as we shall see.

Inclusivity

"It is society that makes it possible for us
to develop ourselves as human beings.
We are part of a group,
as we are all born biologically from a union.
And it is as a part of a group that we yearn to belong."
~Adrienne Clarkson
Belonging: The Paradox of Citizenship

Inclusivity is the characteristic that distinguishes a community from a clique. Cliques are exclusive while communities are inclusive. Groups that are exclusive seek to protect themselves by erecting a barrier to keep non-members out. The members of a clique may experience camaraderie and a feeling of belonging, but it springs from identification with one side of this dichotomy (the members of the group) to the exclusion of the other (everyone else).

Both communities and cliques offer a feeling of comfort and safety, but with a significant difference. In a clique, this feeling is dependent on the acceptance of others; in a community, this feeling comes from your ability to love and accept yourself without the need of outside validation.

The principle of inclusivity applies to cities, towns and countries as well. A community does not fortify borders to keep people out; it draws larger and ever-larger circles to include people in the group. A city can be a community, but it recognizes that it is also part of the larger community of the state or province that is also part of the country's community that is a part of the continent and the global population. Our circles must merge until all the boundaries melt away.

The fact that a community is inclusive does not mean that we become a homogeneous group. Our goal is not to make everyone the same but to come to appreciate, understand and celebrate what makes us different.

Inclusivity refers, as well, to the dynamics within the group. In a community, no one feels excluded. This is why a community discourages pairing. Pairing creates a division, an "us" and "them" *within* the group. Consider the family party where some members sit clustered in a group apart from the others, speaking in hushed tones; the feeling of hearing a conversation go quiet when you approach.

There may come a time when a community must remove a member from the group if their actions threaten the life of the community but the members do not arrive at this decision easily. People in community with one another search for reasons to keep the member in the group while people in a clique look for reasons to cast the member out.

Shared Leadership

"When I am the designated leader
I have found that once a group becomes a community,
my nominal job is over.
I can sit back and relax and be one among many,
for another of the essential characteristics of community
is a total decentralization of authority."
~M. Scott Peck M.D.
The Different Drum: Community Making and Peace

Within this pillar lies the power of community. A community doesn't rely on the leadership of one person but enjoys the talents, experiences, skills and abilities of all its members. In a community, each member offers his or her gifts when they are needed, and, in time, the community comes to know who is best suited to contribute in each situation.

A group of all leaders is richer and more diverse than a group with just one leader. In a community, there is no power struggle, no "party line", and no person is greater or lesser than anyone else. A group that has evolved into community recognizes that they are stronger if the best leader for the present issue is leading.

In a community, the sharing of leadership is standard. What a relief this is to the ones who typically carry the burden of leadership. No one has skills in all areas. In a community, there is someone to step in with answers when the one currently leading doesn't have them. Because of their awareness of their identity as leaders in a group, the members of a community will care about the dynamics of the group, noticing when something is "off" or the spirit is lagging. It takes a group to maintain a community, and it should be that way: A group managed by one or two people is an organization, not a community.

This type of group dynamic, lacking shared leadership, usually falls apart when the ones who are maintaining it leave.

A community is not a democracy. It is not a system defined by ranking, authority, and hierarchical status. It's a place where everyone contributes their thoughts, ideas, and feelings, and, as a group, come to a consensus, an outcome far superior to a decision made by the taking of a vote, or by a decision an individual can achieve. A community is not a hierarchy like a pyramid; the shape of a community is a circle.

I recently visited the council chambers of a nearby city. The plush chairs for the mayor, the city manager and the city clerk, sit on a platform. Just below them, flanking left and right are the chairs of the elected representatives. Together, these chairs look down on a row of not-so-plush seats set upon the floor, the places for the staff members. Along the perimeter of the room are hard plastic, folding chairs for citizens who attend the meetings.

The quality and arrangement of the seats clearly communicates the top-down distribution of power. It also indicates a thinking that is lacking and detrimental to the "community" the council serves. For instance, shouldn't citizens who attend the meetings be made to feel as if they are as welcome as the staff and elected officials?

In a community, we know that we are all in this together and that together we are stronger. This awareness inspires us to actively seek out the feedback, experience, and opinions of many people. A community does not close ranks to hoard the decision-making power among the elite of the group. In a real community, there is no elite.

Collaboration

"Innovation comes from teams
more often
than from the lightbulb moments
of lone geniuses....
As brilliant as many inventors of the Internet and computer were,
they achieved most of their advances
through teamwork."
~Walter Isaacson
The Innovators: How a Group of Hackers, Geniuses, and Geeks
Created the Digital Revolution

In a community, the members have learned to communicate exceptionally well; they care enough about one another to listen. All decision-making goes more smoothly once the group has evolved into a community. There is a reason for this.

Rick Hanson, neuropsychologist and the author of *Hardwiring Happiness; The New Brain Science of Contentment, Calm, and Confidence* says we have three core needs: safety, satisfaction, and connection. Three operating systems support these core needs: to avoid harm, to approach rewards and attach to others. He explains that our brains are in a responsive mode when these needs are met. In a community, we feel safe, satisfied and connected. And when a group is responsive, *"...it can still have misunderstandings, bumps, and conflicts, but they're handled in a responsive way."*

Consider, for a moment, how this idea applies when expanded. If, in our relationships with citizens and governments of other countries, we felt safe, satisfied and connected, how very different would our global relations be?

A community is the ideal collaborative vehicle because the quality of communication among the members makes it viable for them to use consensus for decision-making. After grappling with issues through the consensus process, the group can rest assured that the decisions reached are of the highest calibre. It may take longer to arrive at a the consensus process, the group can rest assured that the decisions decision by consensus, but the result is far superior to one reached through the democratic process because not only is the mind-power of many embraced in the process, but when the group comes to a consensus, everyone wins, not just the ones in the majority. We've come to believe that democracy is the best form of government, but majority-ruled governments can go terribly wrong and have. Consensus guards against that. The one dissenting voice may be the sole voice of reason.

Camaraderie

*"Friendship is born
at that moment when one person says to another:
'What! You too?
I thought I was the only one.'"*
~C.S. Lewis

Community, too, begins with this recognition. Like a many-faceted crystal, a community is comprised of many relationships. Community relationships, like friendships, can be challenging, but they are worth the time and energy required to nurture them because having a community can enrich your life like nothing else can.

Dictionaries define camaraderie as a spirit of fellowship, solidarity, mutual trust and friendship, familiarity, sociability and loyalty among members of a group. Camaraderie is usually present in the initial stage of community building when the people come together with the intention of forming a group, so we often believe we are a community when we have only just begun the community building process. But forming a group into a community takes time. It's not like placing a K-cup and a mug into a single-serve coffeemaker and pressing a button; it's like growing, harvesting, roasting and grinding coffee beans and brewing them in a coffee percolator. True camaraderie develops, in part, because of the time the members invest in the community building process.

Camaraderie is where the fun comes in, but community is more than just fun. Studies show that the longest-lived, healthiest and happiest people are those who enjoy meaningful social connections.

Camaraderie is the result of our interconnectedness with our fellow human beings.

Authenticity

"To be nobody but myself-in a world which is doing its best,
night and day, to make me somebody else
means to fight the hardest battle any human can fight,
and never stop fighting."
- e.e. cummings

In a community, the members communicate authentically with one another. This authenticity fosters the growth of empathy. Empathy strengthens the connections among the members, which makes it easier still to communicate authentically.

Mary Gordon, the author of *Roots of Empathy: Changing the World Child by Child*, says, *"Real communication happens at an emotional level. When we share our feelings, opinions, values and deeply held beliefs with one another, we are able to relate as human beings. Authentic communication is supportive to the growth of social and emotional competence and a basis for developing empathy."*

In a community, people develop the courage to be authentic in their communication. It is in our genuine connections with fellow community members that we recognize that "we are all in this together." In other people's stories, we hear echoes of our own. We see the fears, struggles, desires, failures, successes, and we all experience insecurities.

This commitment to authenticity or the lack of it can mean the success or failure of a group's efforts to evolve into a community. Peck wrote: "*...each one of us is responsible for the success of this group...If you are unhappy with the way things are going--and you will be--it is your responsibility to speak up and voice your dissatisfaction rather than simply pick up your marbles and quietly leave.*" Too often, early in the community building process, members keep their doubts and dissatisfactions to themselves. But the failure to express these things can mean the group may not succeed in becoming a community.

It is only through a willingness to be authentic that we co-create a supportive environment so the group can work through the growing pains of the community-building process, and it is our authenticity with the others in the group that makes a community the beautiful place that it is.

Support

"I'll be there for you
When the rain starts to pour
I'll be there for you
Like I've been there before
I'll be there for you
'Cause you're there for me too"
~ The Rembrandts
Theme from the sitcom Friends

A community is a safe place. It is a place where we feel loved, heard, appreciated and accepted for who we are.

Within a community, we are not constrained by conventions. The typical greeting/question, "How are you?" does not need to be met with "Fine" if that is not how we feel. A community supports us completely and accepts all our emotions; positive and negative. A community is a group of people who have transcended their need to help one another, the impulse to tell people what to do to "fix" themselves or their situations. They support one another in the best possible way by offering presence, silence and a willingness to be with one another in their pain. In the embrace of people who offer these gifts, the person can find the strength to face the challenges that life presents.

Summary

Take another look at the pillars.

- **Commitment** - *sets the stage for community building*
- **Inclusivity** - *distinguishes a community from other groups*
- **Shared Leadership** - *makes a community powerful*
- **Collaboration** - *makes a community effective*
- **Camaraderie** - *makes a community your happy place*
- **Authenticity** - *makes a community special*
- **Support** - *gives a community heart*

Have *you* ever been a part of a group where you were accepted and loved *just because you were there?*

When we look closely at the majestic pillars of community, we understand why community is so rare. It is. Ah, but it doesn't have to be that way.

5

The Community Building Process

"Beware of instant community.
Community-making requires time as well as effort
and sacrifice.
It cannot be cheaply bought."
~M. Scott Peck MD
The Different Drum: Community Making and Peace

The vast majority of groups we call communities are *not* communities, not yet. Most are in the first stage of their development.

Groups become communities by evolving through a specific process. Just as it is through a butterfly's struggle to emerge from its cocoon that the butterfly develops the strength necessary to fly, it is the journey through the community building process that forges a group of individuals into an extraordinary body called a community.

The word community brings to mind a feeling of togetherness, kinship, warmth, belonging, support, camaraderie, and meaningful connection. We use the word wistfully because community is something we all long for. How do we go from yearning for a community to membership in a community? First, we need to understand the process that takes us there.

How Groups Become Communities

Groups become communities in one of three ways:

1. **Intentionally** (The Hangout Group).
2. **Organically** (The Neighbourhood, Book Club, Cross Country team and The Market).
3. **Spontaneously**, in response to a crisis (Keepers of Rte 114 and Moncton Strong).

Spontaneous communities form quickly and naturally in response to a crisis. John T. Cacioppo and William Patrick, Authors of *Loneliness; Human Nature and the Need for Social Connection* describe our human tendency to unite in the face of crisis;

"Many of us tend to ignore the collective aspect of social connection much of the time, then find ourselves surprisingly caught up in a group identity when a national emergency occurs, or when there is some insult to the dignity of a class of persons with which we identify."

A crisis unifies people. In a crisis, we treat one another with compassion. Empathy is a given as we are all in the same situation. In the spontaneous community that a crisis precipitates, the members pass quickly, effortlessly, and seamlessly through the stages of the community building process. In the absence of crisis, the process of community building is neither fast, effortless, nor seamless.

Organic communities grow slowly while **Intentional communities** may grow more quickly, but both Intentional and Organic communities evolve through the four recognizable stages of the community building process that Peck identified in *The Different Drum*:

1. Pseudocommunity
2. Chaos

3. Emptiness
4. Community

Pseudocommunity

"The first response of a group...
is most often to try to fake it.
The members attempt to be an instant community
by being extremely pleasant...
and avoiding all disagreement."
~M Scott Peck MD
The Different Drum: Community Making and Peace

When we first come together to form a group, we are in stage one; pseudocommunity. This is a time when we are getting to know one another, so we naturally seek out things we have in common. We make efforts to be agreeable, and everyone is on his or her best behaviour. The intention to form a group is itself unifying and it brings about a feeling of camaraderie. Because of this harmony and camaraderie, a pseudocommunity is often mistaken for a community. Only later, from our position in a community, do we recognize our error; we had mistaken the caterpillar for the butterfly.

Here's the difference; in pseudocommunity, we share things that are easy to share: We are unwilling to be vulnerable. We don't express opinions that differ from those held by others in the group. We tread softly; we employ tact, we hold back. A group of people in pseudocommunity purchases harmony at the expense of authenticity, hiding what they truly feel and who they truly are. And, usually, when we're in pseudocommunity, we aren't even aware that this is what we're doing.

A pseudocommunity is a group of people who know how to conduct themselves in a group setting, who follow the implicit rules (of our culture, of etiquette) and present a facade of amicability despite what lies beneath. Why would people "fake it" like this?

In 1969, John Powell SJ wrote, *Why Am I Afraid to Tell You Who I Am?* I was a teenager when I read this book but I've never forgotten his reply to the question he posed:

> *"I am afraid to tell you who I am*
> *because you may not **like** who I am*
> *and who I am is all I have."*

Who I am is all I have! Vulnerability comes with great personal risk.

In a university social psychology course, I was introduced to the sociological perspective of dramaturgy. The claim of dramaturgy is that we are always wearing masks that suit the various roles we play in our lives. We may play the role of parent, friend, co-worker and spouse all within the space of a day, and we wear different masks for each role, tailoring our performances to our surroundings and the norms of our culture. We do this to find acceptance from the people around us.

The problem with this is that we become trapped within our roles. Have you ever had the experience of going to a school reunion and feeling exactly the way you felt as a teenager, complete with the adolescent insecurities you had back then? Have you ever returned home for the Holidays, and, upon seeing siblings and parents, felt all the old dynamics snap into place? Do you experience the relief of settling into bed at night, without mask or role, simply being who you are?

It's not surprising that most of what passes for community today are groups of people hiding behind their masks and playing their roles.

If Powell's premise and the theory of dramaturgy are correct, no one knows who we are because no one actually *sees* us: We are only our authentic selves in solitude. After playing these roles for so many years, perhaps we don't even know ourselves who we are.

In a community, we can *be who we are*. And if we are still discovering who we are, our community can support us on this journey.

We are all imperfect human beings in various stages of the process of learning to be okay with that. We all deal with the conditioning of our childhoods, struggling to come into wholeness, authenticity and self-love. We all want to be successful, to feel safe, to be happy and healthy. We all want to feel special; loved for who we are. We all have insecurities, fears, and dreams. In pseudocommunity, however, we're not talking about these things on a meaningful level.

It's not that we intend to be deceitful; we just want to get along with everyone and maybe we are a little bit afraid. But we can't connect authentically with others if we are concealing our differences from them; we can only form these connections when we are willing to find the courage to reveal them, to be who we are even if who we are is different from those around us.

How can we tell when our group is in pseudocommunity? It feels a little boring as if something is missing. We speak in theoretical terms rather than personal ones. We make blanket statements and philosophical ones. We hide behind a third-person narrative rather than risking a first-person one saying, *"Everyone knows..."*, rather than *"I feel..."*

When we communicate on a surface level, as people in pseudocommunities do, we feel safe, and this lulls us into believing we are a community but we are settling for a pencil outline on paper of what can be a full-colour masterpiece on canvas. If we are going to build a genuine community, we need to risk going deeper. Someone must have the courage to remove his or her mask and be authentic despite the chaos that may ensue.

The Pseudocommunity Trap

The most common obstacle a group of people faces as it attempts to build community is the tendency to become trapped in pseudocommunity. This trap closes on us when we don't realize we are in pseudocommunity, but believe we are already a community. This assumption causes us to believe that something must have gone wrong when conflict arises. This is what Missy experienced when she attempted to build community with a group of her friends.

Missy gathered a group of like-minded women together to support one another on their spiritual journeys. At their gatherings, one member, Jax, dominated the conversation. She kept the attention of the group focused on herself rather than sharing the floor with the others. The girls found themselves spending most of their time together trying to help Jax, who seemed unwilling to help herself.

This irritated Missy. She talked privately with some of the other members about it. They shared her frustration but they were all afraid they would offend Jax if they spoke frankly to her about this issue. Finally, the group disbanded as a way of removing Jax. Later, the others tried to carry on, but by then the spirit was gone.

Had they been familiar with the community building process and aware they were in pseudocommunity, they would have recognized that they were on the doorstep of chaos. Knowing this, they would have handled the situation differently.

Their fear of confrontation (chaos) stalled and eventually derailed the group's progress. In retrospect, Missy realized she should have taken action at the first feeling of dissatisfaction and trusted that the members could deal with the issue together.

Too often, we believe we are the only one who feels the way we do. It takes courage to speak up when we assume our opinion is different from the opinions of the others in the group. In a way, this fear is justified because if we do speak up, we risk being scapegoated by members who are not yet willing to face what they feel. Yet, when we take that chance, our actions may inspire others to share how they feel too.

Characteristics of Pseudocommunity

- rule-following; hiding what's authentic beneath what's socially acceptable
- hesitancy; we do not yet want to reveal the deepest of our fears and insecurities; we won't risk authenticity or vulnerability
- politeness and excessive smiling when someone talks for too long or tries to "help" or heal rather than listening and accepting that everyone has their own way to find their solutions
- apprehension; not knowing where we stand with others in the group
- boredom; we wonder what we're doing there, our mind wanders
- conformity; a "perfect" sense of agreement without a dissenting voice, even when we know not everyone agrees

If the group stays together, it will naturally find its way into chaos in time. The honeymoon doesn't last forever, nor do our efforts to be on our best behaviour when behaving means denying our authenticity.

~~~~~

The Hangout Group had been meeting every second week for nearly two years. We were always happy to see one another and we had a lot of fun together, but I knew we were not a community yet. Something was missing. I could feel it, but I wasn't sure what I should do about it so I waited. Then came the day I told them that I was writing a book about community building, and unwittingly cast the group into chaos...

Chaos

"Chaos is not just a state,
it is an essential part of the process
of community development."
~M. Scott Peck MD
The Different Drum: Community Making and Peace

Chaos feels like failure. We believe we are getting along just fine but suddenly there is disruption, upheaval and confusion. Chaos often descends upon the group just when the members begin to feel comfortable with one another and begin to tentatively remove their masks. It can start when a member makes a statement that others disagree with, and a heated discussion ensues. The polite behaviour of pseudocommunity fades away. After the (albeit artificial) harmony of pseudocommunity, this doesn't feel good at all.

Chaos is the stage when we are bold enough to expose our differences, something that comes with the risk of vulnerability. Speaking out requires courage because our thoughts and ideas might be met with opposition. Because most of us don't know how to handle confrontation, we attempt to avoid it. Or perhaps we do share our truth, but after remaining silent for so long, we don't do it tactfully. Chaos is uncomfortable. In this stage, the members feel like something is going wrong; as if the group just isn't working anymore.

Dealing with chaos is as much a personal experience as it is a group one. Until we can face our inner chaos, we will find it difficult to witness its reflection in someone else's life. On a personal level or on a group level, chaos shows us what it is we need to deal with. We can't fix something when we don't even know it's broken. Chaos starts when someone drops their mask, flings the script away, and says what he or she really thinks.

Chaos can take many different forms but essentially, in the stage of chaos, the comfortable feeling we enjoyed in pseudocommunity is suddenly, painfully, absent. When we find ourselves in chaos, we try to retreat to the place where we felt comfortable. Okay, we think, maybe we're not as much alike as we first thought, but if we could all just follow *this* regime, read *this* book, subscribe to *this* belief, we could get back on the same page (that pseudocommunity page). We want to feel we are all the same, so we don't have to deal with our differences and can more easily get along with one another. But usually, by the time we get to chaos, we can't conceal our differences any longer because they've emerged from the shadows and refuse to go back.

Pairing and Chaos

One way the members of a group attempt to avoid chaos is by breaking off into smaller groups of like-minded people. This is called pairing. Pairing may appear innocent, but it can tear a community apart. I had an opportunity to experience this in a failed community building effort many years ago.

A few years after I read The Different Drum*, I decided to try to build a community with a small group of friends. We were still in pseudocommunity and having a lot of fun when we welcomed a new member, Cyndi. At first, everything seemed great, but within a few weeks of her arrival, that all changed. After dating one member of the group, Cyndi pursued another member without ending the relationship with the first, though we urged her to do so. Additionally, she shared stories with some of us, and then she shared contradictory stories with others, but since these conversations happened in smaller groups (pairing), no one was aware of the discrepancies. Then, one day, Cyndi performed a series of manoeuvres that threw our group into chaos from which, despite our many efforts, the group was never able to recover.*

CHARACTERISTICS OF Chaos

- scapegoating - someone is to blame for the mess we're in, often the leader or the first one brave enough to challenge the status quo
- emotional outbursts and indignation - heightened disapproval
- members trying to heal and help one another by telling them what to do
- an attempt to organize the members democratically rather than use the consensus process
- a feeling that everyone is out for himself/herself
- pairing, as an attempt to find harmony with like-minded members of the group

Many groups do not survive the stage of chaos. It takes courage to experience the chaos without backtracking to pseudocommunity. It takes strength to be honest and authentic with people you are just getting to know. The temptation to quit is strong, but if you want to build a community, you have to stay on the community-building path. The way out of chaos is *through* it--and into the next stage; the stage of emptiness.

~~~~~

In the Hangout Group, I read a quote by Scott Peck in an attempt to explain what a real community is. I finished with, "And by the way, we're not a community yet. We're still in pseudocommunity."

*They **protested!** They insisted we had transcended chaos, or maybe we had never needed to go there, that we already were a community. They vehemently disagreed with me - every single person talking at once! I had never seen the group like this! I struggled without success to clarify what I meant. They insisted that we were a community, that it was I who was mistaken. Suddenly it hit me: They were **scapegoating** me! And then I knew that we were in chaos.*

They seized on my every word. I said that even though it was impossible that I'd handled all things that well, no one had ever complained. Corinne said, "What? You want us to lie?" I said we had not revealed our emotional skeletons yet, and Stu offered to share more about an issue he had alluded to earlier about having difficulty with his move to a new place. He was finding it challenging, he said. "No," I said, "that's not an emotional skeleton." I tried to give an example, but it fell flat. We continued to argue about our identity as a pseudocommunity versus a community.

Don pointed out that even though we hadn't revealed emotional skeletons, we had a high level of familiarity because we had all met in the Blogosphere before the first Hangout and knew something of each other because we all read one another's blogs.

Corinne argued that this felt like a community to her. "I'll give you that," I said, "but what if there's more?"

Then, after a time, Stu, ever attentive and thoughtful, reached up, removed his mask and said the thing that ushered us into emptiness...

Emptiness

"Emptiness is the hard part.
It is also the most crucial stage
of community development."
~M. Scott Peck MD
The Different Drum: Community Making and Peace

In emptiness, we find the courage to stop playing our roles. We release our judgments; our ideas of how things should be; our need to control and direct the group. We remove our masks and risk being vulnerable. We empty ourselves of anything that can keep us from moving into community with the members of the group.

We set our solutions aside and allow people to find their own solutions. Emptiness is a time when we realize we may not have all the answers--or that the ones we do have may not be the best ones. We realize that we need to listen. We learn to be silent.

In emptiness, we need to drop our expectations of the others. And we must be willing to let someone feel sad if sad is what they are feeling. We have to have the courage to do the hardest thing - to be with someone in his or her pain. Emptiness is not the triumphant march into the conquered city; it's the slow walk waving a white flag of surrender. Coincidentally, it is often only after the community building leader gives up hope that the group will *ever* evolve into community that the group finds its way there.

You can see that the time spent in pseudocommunity and in chaos are necessary precursors to emptiness. We have needed all this time to lay a foundation; to see what it is we need to empty ourselves of, to recognize that if we have stuck together this long, we will surely make it to the end of the road.

CHARACTERISTICS OF Emptiness

- a relinquishing of pre-conceived notions, judgments, expectations and the need to control
- a fear of losing something we hold dear
- a feeling of giving up
- a ceasing of the performance, a dropping of the masks, courage to just be who we are
- a feeling of quitting that feels more like sweet surrender.

If a group has the courage to experience emptiness, it quickly moves into community.

~~~~~

The Hangout Group had been challenging my claim that we were not yet a community when Stu broke in, "What's really going on is my partner berated me today for not getting certain things cleaned up and organized, asking why it wasn't done and finishing with, 'You don't work.'"

Everyone became quiet. In the silence, I could feel the support that Stu was receiving from the group. This was an emotional skeleton: This was something real. In sharing it, Stu had transported us to a different place. No one attempted to rescue him. We felt his pain, and we stood in solidarity with him. We were in emptiness and community was but a breath away.

Community

"When I am with a group of human beings
committed to hanging in there
through both the agony and the joy of community,
I have a dim sense that I am participating in a phenomenon
for which there is only one word.
I almost hesitate to use it.
The word is 'glory'"
~M Scott Peck MD
The Different Drum: Community Making and Peace

Months later, when I asked the members of the Hangout Group when they felt we had come into community, they all referred to that Hangout when I had told them we were in pseudocommunity.

I asked if they felt our group was different from other groups they belonged to and if it was, *how* it was different.
Corinne said that even though none of us have met in person, she feels close to this group, that it is therapeutic for her to be here. She had missed most of the meetings over the summer, and she said it was a palpable gap for her, that being here both grounded her and lifted her up.

Stu said the value for him was the different perspectives it offers and the feeling that the group has his back. He said he felt connected to everyone. Here, he feels able to relax, and trust.

Don seconded that, saying he felt he didn't have to filter his thoughts here or put on performance of any kind. He could share what he was thinking without qualifying his views by producing a set of credentials. *"I'm just me here."* Don said he found it easy to trust and relax here where there are no agendas, no competition and no one "playing false."

Veronica pointed to the flow, camaraderie and a cohesive yet heterogeneous mix of people. She said that after the meetings, she had to take time and ground herself because everyone raised the vibration of everyone else at the meetings.

Jamie, who was one of the original members, said it was *"Great!"* *"Awesome!"* He said there was no pressure here, and he enjoyed coming every week.

For me, community is being with friends who love me, even though they see me for who I am. It's a place where I can just be who I am, where I am, at that moment.

In a community, the members know your quirks, and they love you for them; they don't judge you because of them. That's an amazing feeling.

Community Growth and Maintenance

Communities require maintenance, just as marriages and friendships do. After we have evolved into community, we continue to cycle through the four stages again and again, each time moving into more meaningful community with one another. Like a relationship between two newlyweds continues to evolve and deepen over the years, so, too, do the relationships among the members of a community.

We might seem to lose the spirit from time to time, and then we find our way back to it again. For instance, one day we may find ourselves feeling more like a pseudocommunity than a community. And then, as happened at one of our hangouts…

I was so happy it was Hangout Day because I had been having a rough time over the Thanksgiving weekend. I shared how I felt and how I dreaded the thought of going through another Christmas without Alex. At first, everyone peppered me with suggestions as to how I could handle this grief that would torment me anew at Christmastime. We talked and volleyed ideas back and forth. I was saying I don't want to deal with this, and they were telling me that I must and supplying suggestions as to how to do it. (Chaos)

Then Stu said he was sure he spoke for everyone in saying that by their suggestions, they didn't mean to diminish in any way the unimaginable pain I was feeling, that he cared about me deeply and wanted me to be okay. As he said this, his eyes filled with tears. (Emptiness)

I stared at the screen, feeling blessed to be in the presence of so much love. I looked at the faces of Rose and Corinne and they, too, gazed at Stu in love and gratitude. (Community)

To not feel the need to apologize for becoming emotional and to have no one try to stop or rescue you; that's a deeper level of community than we had yet experienced. The evolution of our group into community had not finished when we reached stage four for the first time. It was just that; the first of many times we would grow together as a community.

A good marriage requires work; a real friendship does too. Why would a community be any different? The beauty of community maintenance, as opposed to community building, is that it's a trek down a familiar path, the one we took to get there, so if we get lost, we can always find our way again.

Summary of the Four Stages

Pseudocommunity - a structured, rule-based, polite phase where cultural norms and expectations are clear, and everyone conforms to them without questioning them.

Chaos - it begins when someone says, *"Wait a minute!"* It's the stage where someone shares authentically, and, deliberately or inadvertently, challenges the status quo.

Emptiness - a time of giving up, setting down the tools, weapons, masks and giving up the fight. It's a quiet phase of surrender, self-awareness and complete suspension of judgment.

Community - the transformation.

These are the four stages of community building, the path where all groups that evolve into community travel. Recognizing where we are in the process proves invaluable. But it isn't enough to simply understand the community building process: We need to know how to lead a group of people down this path.

6

How to Lead a Group of People into Community

"Life at its best
exists in cooperative, sharing,
and balanced relationships
with other lives.
This is the interdependence
we call belonging."
~ Adrienne Clarkson
Belonging: The Paradox of Citizenship

The role of the community-building leader is to facilitate authentic, meaningful communication among the members of a group. Community building, in essence, is achieved by talking. There are several "Community Building Conversation Starters" in the Appendix that you can use to guide your group in discussion. First, let's look at the role of the community building leader.

The Gardener

A community-building leader is like a gardener. He or she;
1. prepares the soil
2. plants the seeds
3. waters the garden
4. weeds and protects the garden
5. waits for it to grow

STEP 1
Prepare the Soil:
Create an Environment for Community Building

The first step is to focus on what we want. We need to spend time thinking about our vision for the group. Focusing on our vision may be the most important thing we do because our intention shapes our attitude, sparks our enthusiasm, and raises our vibration. When we imagine what we want, that energy will attract people and situations to help us manifest our vision.

As the leader, this is how we create an environment for community building.

STEP 2
Plant the Seeds:
Introduce the Concept of Community and Engage Others to Take Part in the Experience

Now we move into action to find people who will join us in a community building exercise. To build a community either online or offline, first we can reach out to people we know well. We inspire them with the idea of gathering regularly with a group of individuals for "a community building experience." Initially, all we need is three or four people who will commit to the exercise. Ask everyone to invite two or three of their friends. It's not important that we are well acquainted with all the people who will join us: The experience can be even more fun with people we don't know at all.

In the Appendix you'll find steps for setting up a Facebook account and more to create a place to build a community online and to prepare a way to stay in touch with people if you are building a community offline.

STEP 3
Water the Garden:
Host the Meetings

To prepare for the first meeting, we begin by thinking about our purpose for gathering. Are we a church group aspiring to create more meaningful connections among parishioners, or a teacher building community in the classroom, or a group of people building community so we can have fascinating discussions about life, or are we simply a group of individuals who want to have the experience of community? We keep this in mind as we prepare for the first meeting.

No matter what other goals we have for gathering, a project, for instance, it's essential to build community first because once we are a community, everything else will run more smoothly.

The First Meeting

At the first meeting, we introduce the group to the concept of community using the analogy of house and home found in Chapter 4, so everyone will have a sense of what it is we are doing. We can also print out the seven pillars of a community, as a set of parameters; something to refer to when needed. We engage their cooperation, enthusiasm, and commitment to building community together.

Sifting through the Community Building Conversation Starters in the Appendix, we see if there is a Group-Specific one that suits our group, or we can use one as a model to create our own. Alternately, we can use the first Community Building Conversation Starter to both spark discussion and to further introduce the concept of community to the group.

Moderating the Meetings

At the first meeting with a large group, pair each person with someone they don't know and get them to interview one another. Suggest a few interview questions that are relevant to the group. For instance, for a mom's group, questions about how many children they have, names and ages, and add a question like this: What is your biggest challenge as a mom? Then, after giving them a few minutes, have each person introduce their partner to the group. This exercise is an excellent ice-breaker.

Encourage everyone to be on time but flow with the latecomers, trusting that there are no accidents, only synchronicities.

Allow time for a little friendly chit chat as members first arrive. Introduce any latecomers to the others.

Ask the first question and let the conversation flow. As much as possible, ensure that everyone has a chance to respond to the question before moving on to the next one: If we don't get through all the questions, we can continue the discussion at the next meeting.

Use silence. If we are too quick to respond when someone finishes talking, we won't leave space for others to add to the discussion. Sometimes, all it takes is a pause to allow a meaningful response to come through. Notice how we often feel compelled to fill the silence. If we are comfortable with silence, eventually the members will take their cues from us, and the conversation will be relaxed and flowing.

Be careful not to monopolize. We need to be aware that the role of moderator is different from that of a presenter. A moderator facilitates conversation among the members of the group and steps back to let it unfold.

Interrupt. If someone is speaking at length or has gone off the topic in such a way as to derail the conversation, we may, at times, have to interrupt and clarify the question. If we don't do this, others who rely on the moderator to handle this may become frustrated or bored. Though the members of the group will eventually assume a mutual leadership role in this area, initially it will be up to the leader.

Draw in the quiet one. Make sure each person is invited into the conversation. In the Hangout Group, I often notice Rose is looking down quietly. When I call on her, I learn that she has been listening and taking note of her thoughts so she can share them later.

Resist the need to control. Leading a group into community is much different from any other leading we do in life. We need to be discerning and contemplative, taking the time to understand the situation thoroughly before responding.

Finally, we shouldn't be hard on ourselves. Peck wrote that often it was when he had given up on a group that the members came into community. I have experienced this too.

When we first meet with a group of people to build community, we don't know who will be the first one brave enough to share an opposing view. We don't know who will be the one to reach out to the silent one who has wisdom to share but hesitates to speak up. We don't know who will be the one to talk openly about a topic that needs to be raised. These are treasures we discover along the way.

STEP 4
Weed and protect the garden:
Be vigilant and responsive to threats to the group

A gardener needs to protect the garden from weeds that steal the nutrients from the plants, from bugs and small burrowing animals that would attack the roots and eat the young seedlings. Just as a gardener keeps a vigilant eye on his or her garden, a community-building leader pays attention to the interactions within the group. We need to be aware that if the process is to unfold, we may have to take action to protect the group from "weeds", "bugs" and "small burrowing animals".

Looking out for the group means noticing if "pairing" is happening, for instance, and pointing out any unproductive negativity. It means upholding our vision and perhaps even reminding the group of the goal of the gatherings. An example of this is what happened when Justin Trudeau introduced his cabinet days after he was elected Prime Minister of Canada in 2015. A reporter asked why it was so important to him that his cabinet be gender balanced. His reply clearly reinforced his leadership goals of inclusivity and shared leadership: *"Because it's 2015,"* he said.

STEP 5
Wait
Allow the Community Building Process to Unfold

This may be the hardest step: We have to be patient and allow the group to evolve naturally into community. Community building is an organic process. Had I pushed the group into chaos any sooner than I inadvertently did, the outcome might have been very different.

In this step, we recognize where the group is in the community building process and gradually introduce the members to the stages *when necessary* so they will understand what is happening and begin to share responsibility for the health and evolution of the community.

One of the greatest assets of the community-building leader is faith. Like the gardener, who, though anxious to see the first sprouts appear knows the folly of digging up seeds to see why they are taking so long to germinate, the community building leader learns to become adept at waiting while still doing what he or she can to guide the group.

We need to relax and trust the process. If we assume too powerful a leadership role, we will not allow the process to unfold naturally, as it should, yet if we are too passive, that growth may be thwarted.

Patience is key. The community building process is not a superhighway; it's the long and delightful scenic route.

LORI GOSSELIN

7

The Community Building Tools and Life

*"It does not matter how slowly you go
as long as you do not stop."*
~ Confucius

Many times in life, we travel through the stages of the community building process. We do this not only with our groups but also in relationships with a friend or a partner -- and in the relationship with ourselves.

An understanding of the seven pillars that define community and an awareness of the community building process is invaluable as we face life's challenges. These tools can help us to understand our relationships and shine a light upon the next step on the path.

Traveling the Path with Friends and Partners

A group of two people can become a community. We begin the relationship in the first stage, **pseudocommunity**. This is the honeymoon phase, a time of newness and harmony when we see only the best in one another. We are anxious to please, revealing only the positive, appealing parts of ourselves. At this early stage in the relationship, everything seems perfect.

We remain in stage one until conflict arises when someone sees something that isn't so perfect. This upsets the dynamic. We begin to recognize that we don't agree on everything. We are different. The relationship is not as perfect as it had seemed. The honeymoon is over. We are in **chaos**.

Chaos in a relationship is painful but it also signifies hope: It means we've left pseudocommunity behind. No matter when this happens, early in the relationship or years later, we have an opportunity to take the relationship to a deeper, more authentic place.

But upon encountering chaos, we often attempt to retreat into pseudocommunity. We don't like the conflict of chaos, we want that honeymoon feeling, but we don't know how to get it back without sacrificing our authenticity. Often that looks like this: *If you can't love me for who I am and I can't be other than who I am, then what do we do? Where do we go from here?* We may oscillate between chaos and pseudocommunity many times before we have the courage to stay in chaos and face it.

A retreat to pseudocommunity isn't the answer. Chaos will reveal the things we need to release in order to move forward; our expectations, our disappointments, our need for control. Once we know what we are dealing with, it is time to move into the silence of **emptiness.**

Emptiness means listening without judgment, searching for a deeper understanding, waiting. It means retiring to a quiet place and letting our thoughts flow freely without judging them. We might choose to step away from the problem to let it settle so that we can make space for new insights. Emptiness demands that we take responsibility for, and deal with, the issues that have come to light in the chaos. The answers will find us in the silence of emptiness. So, we wait.

Human beings are complex. We can't understand another person without an enormous amount of effort. To complicate this, we grow and evolve constantly. When we look at the people we know best, we tend to see what we saw yesterday. Our expectations trap people; it's difficult to rise above other people's expectations of us. Emptiness can be a gift we give to our loved ones on a daily basis: *I will see you with fresh eyes every day.*

If we are able to empty ourselves of our expectations, judgements, preconceptions, and demands, and still maintain our authenticity, we will find our way to **community**.

In relationships with friends and partners, we may cycle many times through the stages, each time going deeper and more fully into community with one another. Finding ourselves in chaos after many years, though scary, is not cause for alarm. It is an opportunity to grow even closer.

Community Building and Emotional Healing

The four stages of community building are not just a process of bringing people together in a meaningful way; they are a tool for healing the personal issues we face on our journey through life.

When we are facing a personal issue, we first identify the stage we're in. It looks like this: Am I pretending the problem doesn't exist, that I'm not upset or angry about it? Am I smiling while I stuff down my feelings? I may be in **pseudocommunity**, weighed down by age-old issues, playing the role I assumed in childhood.

How do I feel about the issue? I have to be willing to go into the chaos of my feelings to see and understand what's there. **Chaos** demands that I face it honestly. Allowing and honoring my feelings, even if they don't feel good right now, is preferable to a pseudocommunity that denies them, because chaos, even the chaos of emotional turmoil, represents a forward motion; hope. Ignoring my feelings won't make them go away just as pretending that all is well won't make a pseudocommunity a community.

Eventually, if I stay in the chaos long enough, I will find my way to **emptiness**. Perhaps I safely vent my emotions; in honoring them, I am able to release them. We never see anything, past or present, except through the lenses of our belief systems. It was what we told ourselves about what happened that was responsible for the majority of the hurt we felt. As adults, we can examine our beliefs to see if they still serve us, and release them when they don't.

When I have successfully released the feelings, I come to know what the feelings were really about, and with that clarity I am liberated. The distorting lenses are gone. I walk in authenticity. I move into a wholesome **community** within myself about the issue.

The Community Building Path and Grief

When we are grieving, we move through the first three stages of the community building process, again and again. At times, we may feel we're not making any progress. Here we are at Christmas again, with endless Christmas carols resurrecting all the happy memories that hurt so much to remember. But the seasons that cycle around year after year help us to heal the many layers of grief, gently and gradually, as we are able to do. Here is how I journeyed through the grief of losing my son.

Pseudocommunity
In the early days after Alex died, I didn't want to leave the house. I found the greatest solace in going to the stockroom in the basement to fill orders for our business, orders that continued to come through our website as if my whole world hadn't fallen apart. The action of filling the orders helped me; it provided an activity that was blessed, ordinary routine. I needed that. I was hiding; in my home, in my basement, in the first phase of my grief, reaching for and clinging to any semblance of normalcy.

Chaos

But chaos comes in the quiet moments when distractions are at bay; it comes during the holidays which sweep our routine aside. It seeps in on a quiet Saturday morning when we don't have work to occupy us. Pain is the harbinger of chaos. We try to avoid pain by reverting to the familiar, comforting routine. We want to hide in the basement where our grief can't find us.

We can resist the chaos, and at times, we *must*, as I did in the earliest days, but eventually we have to face it. Chaos is the lump in your throat that isn't going to go away. You can choke it back as much as you like, but you know you're going to cry. It's just a matter of time.

So, we move unwillingly into the chaos. We find ourselves there as we approach the second Christmas and the third Christmas, wondering how it can still hurt as much as it did the first year. We want to escape what is so painful, but there doesn't seem to be any escape. So, we embrace the pain and the grief like a mug of hot cocoa on a cold winter day. We take comfort in the warmth of the tears, the sound of our wailing (a healing sound; a sound therapy), and through this action, we make our way into emptiness.

Emptiness

In emptiness, we begin to approach acceptance, perhaps brought on by the exhaustion that comes from trying so hard to hang on to the old reality, a reality that no longer is and will never be again. In this stage, we recognize this. In this stage, we begin to let go.

With the surrender of emptiness comes peace. It was in accepting that we would never again be the precious "four of us", that I felt a strange relief. The pain of wanting--so desperately--something I could never again have was lessened, at least for a time.

Each time I move through the stages, I make advancements through my grief, however small. With each cycle, the journey deepens and the healing solidifies more and more.

This framing of the journey through grief provides clues as to how we can support someone who is grieving. We can be willing to listen to the emotions, which need to be heard. We can be the witness who assures the person they are not alone; the only healing salve to the pain and loneliness of grief. We can recognize the stage the person is in. Is he reaching for routine, soldiering on as if the old reality can be maintained? He is in pseudocommunity. Is she raging or weeping at the injustice of the loss and fearing that life will never again be good again? She is struggling with chaos.

Awareness of this process, and of the unfathomable value as a witness who offers presence, empathy and affirmation, empowers us to just be present, to be aware and to allow the process to unfold.

The Path and Our Evolution Through Life

Our journey from the crib to the grave can be understood through the lenses of the community building process. In early childhood, we are subject to rules and control of those who take care of us; our parents and teachers. We learn to follow the rules; we do as we're told. As long as we are "good girls and boys" everything seems just fine. This hierarchy of control ensures that things stay copacetic. This is the **pseudocommunity** of childhood where we learn to conceal our feelings and pretend to be the person we need to be in order to gain acceptance and love.

When do we move into **chaos** on the path of our personal evolution? Ideally, it should happen around the age of two. Enlightened parents celebrate this display of the will of their child. But we don't all reach chaos at the age of two. Some of us don't say that first adamant "No!" until we hit our teen years, or our thirties--or even beyond. Chaos can be a time of anger because anger is a precursor of the reclaiming/claiming of personal power. The "Wait a minute!" of chaos manifests as rebellion, uncooperative behaviour, or passive aggressive behaviour. Perhaps it resembles a "mid-life crisis". A crisis is chaos. Sometimes, the advent of chaos can make us angry for many, many years, as we oscillate between chaos and pseudocommunity until we can work our way to emptiness.

Emptiness feels like a deep sigh. It's a decision to claim--and be-- who we are. It's a state of forgiveness, and of letting go. Emptiness is a time of observing without reacting, gathering as much understanding as possible and releasing what no longer serves us. It's a time of determination and excitement because of what now lies in our sights. In emptiness we don't have all the answers but we recognize that we have come one step closer to finding them, that they are not far away. Such is the peace of emptiness.

Do we ever reach community in our evolution? I don't know. People like Eckhart Tolle and the Dalai Lama seem to have achieved this but even they would tell us that it is the journey that matters, and not the destination.

The community building process can offer signposts to guide us. Are we still following the rules to gain acceptance from the people we assume hold power over us? (Pseudocommunity) Are we angry about our perceived lack of personal power? (Chaos) Are we sitting in the aftermath of the storm we've just weathered? (Emptiness) Are we aware of our innate right to be who we are and to love ourselves unconditionally? (Community)

Many times in life we travel down the community building path, in relation to our personal growth and healing and in relationships with others. The community building process is a precious map that allows us to recognize where we are on the path so we know what steps to take next.

A Relationship Checklist

The seven pillars, which show us where to focus our attention as we move through the community building stages in relationships, can be particularly helpful in long-term relationships of two. Remember that the absence of even one pillar is a deal-breaker. Imagine a marriage in which you were no longer nurturing your relationship and the camaraderie that you enjoyed when you first came together is diminished. Or picture a relationship where one person holds all the power in a situation that affects both of you.

Consider your relationship as it pertains to the seven pillars to see which aspects may need to be strengthened.

Commitment: Are you both firmly committed to the relationship?

Inclusivity: Do you embrace and accept all aspects of one another?

Shared Leadership: Do you share in the decision-making?

Collaboration: Do you use consensus to make decisions made that affect the relationship?

Camaraderie: Do you take time to have fun together?

Authenticity: Are you able to be yourself in this relationship?

Support: Do you both feel completely supported by one another as you pursue your dreams and face life's inevitable trials?

Bonus check-point: Communication *Do you **tell** one another how you feel;* your commitment to one another, your love of all aspects of one another, your true thoughts about the decisions you share, your feelings about the things you do for fun? Do you dare to be yourself because you feel supported by the other? "Consensus" should be a part of the marriage vows and community should always, always be the goal.

8

Why Community Matters

"...Numerous other studies
have supported the medical researchers' intuition
that social cohesion matters,
not just in preventing premature death,
but also in preventing disease and speeding recovery."
~ Robert D. Putnam
Bowling Alone: The Collapse and Revival of American Community

Ample current research shows that community matters to us very much. As human beings, we are wired for community. Community is far more than a group of people who enjoy spending time together. Community is the very way we survive as a species.

Everyone wants to be happy. We may each produce a different list of things that we believe will make us happy, but there is one common factor; we need someone to share that happiness with us. If we won thirty million dollars, or were awarded the Nobel Peace Prize, our joy would be short-lived if we had to experience it in solitude.

In addition to the need to have someone to share our joy, we need people who we are closely connected to at times when we are struggling in life. Knowing we are supported and loved by our tribe separates the survivors from those who submit to despair. The happiest people on the planet are those who have a strong social network in their lives.

Science shows that when we expect something to happen the brain changes its physiological state in anticipation. I've seen evidence of this in people who book a Reiki treatment in a panic and then are perfectly calm by the time they arrive at my door. Just having an expectation of receiving support makes us begin to feel better and when we are part of a community, we know there is always someone there to support us.

Our health, too, is impacted by the presence of our tribe. Lissa Rankin, the author of *Mind Over Medicine: Scientific Proof That You Can Heal Yourself,* reports after extensive research into the science behind the placebo effect, that the body can heal all on its own when it assumes a relaxation response as opposed to a stressed, fight or flight one: This is a vital and significant discovery: When we have a supportive community, we know we never have to face difficult times alone.

A Healing Place for Emotional Wounds

"Oh, the comfort, the inexpressible comfort
of feeling safe with a person;
having neither to weigh thoughts nor measure words,
but to pour them all out, just as they are,
chaff and grain together,
knowing that a faithful hand will take and sift them,
keep what is worth keeping, and then,
with a breath of kindness,
blow the rest away."
~Dinah Maria Mulock Craik

A community is like the perfect friendship described in this poem. It's a place where we know we can safely share our thoughts and feelings, pretty and ugly, knowing they will be received by people who genuinely care about us. When we feel heard, we find the strength and courage we need to deal with the challenges life presents. Imagine how amazing it feels to have not one person but an entire group of people to support you on the emotional journey of life.

Dr Allan Abbass, foremost expert in attachment theory and Author of *Reaching Through Resistance: Advanced Psychotherapy Techniques*, said in an interview that he is astonished to meet with people in their sixties and beyond who are overcome by the compassion of the therapist who asked them how they felt. I noticed this in my Reiki practice when at the end of a treatment, a young woman said, *"No one has ever asked me that before."* When I asked her what she meant, she said, *"No one has ever asked me how I feel."* Community creates a space for healing because it is made up of people willing to ask that question and to care about the person expressing their pain.

We usually respond to the standard greeting, *"How are you?"* by saying, *"I'm fine, thank you, how are you?"* but we all need a place where it is safe to give an authentic answer. My Hangout group has become that place for me.

> *Stu was the first to arrive at the Hangout. "Hi, Lori! How are you?" he asked.*
>
> *I was not doing well. Two days ago was Mother's Day and I spent much of it crying, missing Alex. The next day would have been his twenty-sixth birthday. Then we learned that my nephew had died after a long illness. I was dreading the imminent visit to pay our respects to the family. I felt I had no comfort to bring to them. But how could I say all this to Stu? I thought; I should just give the generic response, "I'm fine, thank you. How are you?"*
>
> *But I didn't.*
>
> *"I'm not doing too well," I said.*
>
> *"Aw!" Stu said, "What's going on?"*

That began an authentic conversation that grounded and strengthened me. Thanks to Stu's empathy and willingness to listen, I realized that I could offer the family my presence and a listening ear without trying to make better something that would not be better for a very long time. This was the gift Stu had given me.

In response to our deepest pain, all anyone can ever offer us is his or her willingness to be with us without needing to make the pain go away. We find a way to heal ourselves in the presence of such a person.

We conform to conventions for a reason. It's not practical, nor would it be considered mentally sound, to spill out all our problems in response to every *"How are you?"* But how valuable it is to have a place where we can process the sorrows and frustrations of our lives; a place to offload our burdens for a time *"...knowing that a faithful hand will take and sift them..."* Community is such a place.

A Witness to Our Lives

"Why is it, do you think, that people get married? ...
Because we need a witness to our lives...
In a marriage, you're promising to care about everything;
the good things, the bad things,
the terrible things, the mundane things -
all of it, all the time every day.
You're saying,
'Your life will not go unnoticed because I will notice it.
Your life will not go unwitnessed
because I will be your witness.'"
~ from a scene in the 2004 movie
Shall We Dance

All through grade school as I walked home at the end of the day, I anticipated sharing the events of my day with my mother. She arranged her activities so she would be free when my siblings and I returned from school because she knew we would want to talk with her.
My communities have always been that for me, a place to come home to and share my troubles and my adventures. They are

witnesses to the fact I exist and that my existence matters.

Social Cooperation and Loneliness

"...the driving force
of our advance as a species
has not been our tendency to be brutally self-interested,
but our ability to be socially cooperative."
~John T. Cacioppo and William Patrick
Loneliness; Human Nature and the Need for Social Connection

Little is so painful as the sting of being excluded. Do we not all have memories of our school days when we did not receive a coveted invitation to the birthday party of a popular classmate? We have known this pain, the harbinger of loneliness, of being excluded from the tribe.

We long for the meaningful connections of community with a wordless yearning. Because community is our natural state, what hurts us most is feeling lonely.

Loneliness is an assessment of how we feel no matter how many people are around us. I can be in the midst of a crowd and feel lonely, but it is rare that I feel lonely when I have a community, even when I am not with the group. Some of my most poignant experiences of community were times when I was apart from the group yet still felt connected to, and supported by, the people in it.

This characteristic of community may come as a relief to the introvert. People in a community do not have to spend all their time together to maintain the bond. My community experiences include groups that have met at intervals of once a week to once a month to once a year. Part of the power of community is that even when the members are not together, we know they would move from "there" to "here" without hesitation if we needed them.

The Next Evolutionary Leap

"Because early humans were more likely to survive
when they stuck together,
evolution reinforced the preference
for strong human bonds
by selecting genes that support pleasure in company
and produce feelings of unease
when involuntarily alone."
~John T. Cacioppo and William Patrick
Loneliness; Human Nature and the Need for Social Connection

In his book, *Spontaneous Evolution,* Bruce Lipton says our next evolutionary leap will be into community and by that leap we will preserve our species. He claims that we have the problems we face today because we have lost the nature of community.

When evolution reinforces a preference, it is called a "socially adaptive" trait. It is socially adaptive to seek connection with our fellow human beings; it is in our very genes. In our cave-dwelling past, it was dangerous to be alone. To be a part of a group ensured our safety and survival. Those who evolved are those who learned to collaborate.

We need community. Cacioppo and Patrick write, *"We need to remember not only the ways in which loneliness heightens our threat surveillance and impairs our cognitive abilities, but also the ways in which the warmth of connection frees our minds to focus on whatever challenges lie before us."*

Our best chance of survival in these tumultuous times, too, lies in community.

When we speak of community, we are talking about our personal happiness, and our ability to thrive in the face of adversity. However, much more than this is at stake. We are no longer merely talking about the survival of the tribe: We're talking about the preservation of our species.

We Yearn for Community

"Something deep inside us knows
that together we are more.
We can accomplish more together,
we are safer together,
and we can find greater comfort
when we are together....
Being in community
is our natural state."
~Paul Born
Deepening Community; Finding Joy Together in Chaotic Times

How often we reach for community unaware! We enjoy community vicariously by watching television shows like *Friends* where a group of people gather at a coffee house and share their lives. We join the tribe of *Seinfeld, Cheers, How I Met Your Mother, Modern Family, The Big Bang Theory* and many others, to receive our daily dose of community. We become involved with the characters, enjoying the close bonds, the camaraderie, the mutual support, the sense of belonging they experience. We like the way they care about one another.

The sitcom, *Community*, provides an example of a group evolving into community. Though the name of the sitcom seems to refer to the community college, the show is really about the dynamics of a diverse group of students who come to care about one another. In the diverse group of students who come to care about one another. In the first episode, the group moves through the four stages of the community building process. They will continue to cycle through the process in the following episodes as they move more deeply into community.

It isn't just sitcoms that provide our daily dose of community. We are also drawn to the communities on television series and movies. The show *Blue Bloods* gives us a sense of community in a family, where nearly every show includes a supper table scene of four generations gathering in good will and support. A briefly run Hallmark series called *Signed, Sealed; Delivered* presents the beautiful interplay of a small group of very different people growing into a community.

We celebrate the moment when a group of people come to care about one another despite their differences. These are the moments that touch us; they strike a familiar chord within us. Even their theme songs speak of community, the soundtracks setting the tone as we settle in to watch the shows.

Why Community Matters to Me

"Good friends are like stars.
You don't always see them,
But you know they're always there."
~Author Unknown

My Hangout Group is comprised of a very diverse group of people. We number only seven, yet we seven represent four religions, two continents, four countries and four cultures, and our ages span four decades. In our time together, we have come to know and appreciate what makes us different. We know that Stu is not afraid to show his emotions or express empathy. We know that Don will provide humour, but he will not hesitate to disagree with everyone in the group. Corinne sees the bright side of any situation and is brilliant at sharing it. Jamie has a favourite phrase he pulls out in challenging circumstances, "It happens," he says, with such Zen calm. Veronica is able to laugh no matter what is going on in her life. She's solid, like a boulder in the rapids. Rose hears everything at a deeper level. She will offer you the truth even when it's hard to hear.

In the time we've been together, every single one of us has faced major life issues; divorce, career crisis, moves, loss of a brother, a son, a mother, illness, and break-ups and throughout it all, we've been there for one another. I wouldn't dare imagine how I would have survived the events of the past few years of my life without the support of this community.

Summary

On a personal level, community not only completes our lives; it enriches them like nothing else can. Community is our natural state. This is why, in times of crisis, community grows spontaneously. But in ordinary times, too, we need meaningful connections with our fellow passengers on the journey of life. Social media has arrived on the scene just in time to respond to this need.

9

Social Media and Community Building

The Digital Connection

*"What shapes our interaction
more than any other factor
is attachment,
whether we interact in person,
by mail, by phone,
or through the Internet.
The technology may be new,
but the dynamics
are as old as humankind."*
~Gordon Neufeld, Ph.D and Gabor Mate, MD
Hold On to Your Kids; Why Parents Need to Matter More Than Peers

Human beings are social creatures. We find and seize opportunities to connect with people, even if we do so from the privacy of our homes in front of our computer screens or smart phones. Neufeld and Mate say, *"It is unsurprising..... that the amazing technology originally designed for information has been pressed, instead, into the service of seeking connection."*

Many are quick to dismiss the authenticity of the relationships formed with people met online, but meaningful connections are a product of communication, not of the mode we use to communicate. The calibre and depth of the relationships are up to us. Online, especially on my blog, I've connected with people from all over the world with whom I'd trust some of my deepest secrets, and *I've never met these people in person.*

Should digital connections replace in-person interaction? No, but they can be good adjuncts to them. And sometimes they are valuable substitutes. Consider, for instance, my niece whose husband plays professional football. Shortly after their son was born, her husband had to go away for two months. The father's absence challenged the bond between father and son so they used video chatting via FaceTime, daily, to shrink the space between them.

We have all seen people interrupt a conversation to tend to the sound of an email or a text. We are rarely without our phones. Our addiction to our gadgets has caused a word to be added to our dictionary *(Nomophobia; the fear of being out of mobile phone contact)*. But why would we reach outside our physical surroundings for connection if we had it right where we were? We wouldn't. In a world craving community, is it possible that we have found a way to have it in our lives?

Our attraction to technology and our still-evolving texting habits are an indication of what is lacking in society today, and of what is needed. The hands that are holding so tightly to our devices are reaching for community.

Technology Under Attack

"Almost every digital tool whether designed for it or not,
was commandeered by humans
for a social purpose:
to create communities, facilitate communication,
collaborate on projects,
and enable social networking."

~Walter Isaacson
*The Innovators: How a Group of Hackers, Geniuses, and Geeks
Created the Digital Revolution*

Social media and the technology we use to access it are under attack. They have been accused of being disruptive, charged with causing depression and social anxiety, and condemned for hurting our culture. But how can they merit such an enormous burden of responsibility? The Internet is the vehicle, but we are in the driver's seat. How we drive it, and how we teach our children to navigate, is *our* responsibility.

Like many children growing up in the sixties, I was held responsible for my actions but thirty years later, this was not the common approach taken by parents or teachers or society at large. When my son was in middle school, a small group of students loitered daily at local restaurants at lunchtime. The school officials responded to complaints from merchants by instituting a policy that prevented all students from leaving school grounds during the lunch break. In doing this, the school assumed responsibility for the students' behaviour rather than teaching the students to be responsible by allowing them to experience the consequences of their actions. Why should the actions of a few be allowed to affect the entire school population and effect change in school policy? This type of response was not an exception. It was the norm.

A generation later, we are "helicopter parents" and "snowplough parents" attempting to childproof the world to keep our children safe. It is not the job of parents to protect children from life; we need to prepare them for it by educating them in their safe and happy navigation through it.

Gordon Neufeld, Ph.D. and Gabor Mate, MD, authors of *Hold On to Your Kids,* say *"There is nothing inherently bad about these devices; the concern is about their use, especially in the hands of our children. When to introduce and when to discourage such use is the question."* We need to prepare young children for social media before we give them that first gadget; we need to educate them so they know how to sail safely in the sea of technology.

This is important because the world today is a technological world. We can't just remove the gadgets from our children; they need to learn how to use technology. Our job is to ensure that they use it in a wholesome way.

We also need to understand the allure that technology holds for us. Our nomophobia is not the problem but the symptom of an issue. The issue is our lack of community.

Propinquity

"In social psychology, propinquity...
(From Latin propinquitas, "nearness")
is one of the main factors leading to interpersonal attraction.
It refers to the physical or psychological proximity between people."
~ Wikipedia

In the past, propinquity was the primary catalyst for community building. In a neighbourhood or a university residence, we tend to form friendships with the people who live near to us. Once we move away, and propinquity is gone, the friendships often dissolve. The digital age adds another layer to the definition of "propinquity". If we have a computer or other gadget and an Internet connection, we can connect with people anywhere in the world where these things exist.

Video conferencing technologies like Google+ Hangouts and Skype have evolved computer-mediated communication into *face-to-face interaction.* The technology that many criticize has made citizens of every country our neighbours and potential members of our next community.

Community Building Online

*"Communication is a fundamental prerequisite
for social and emotional connections.
Telecommunications in general and the Internet in particular
substantially enhance our ability to communicate,
thus it seems reasonable to assume
that their net effect will be to enhance community,
perhaps even dramatically."*
~ Robert D. Putnam
Bowling Alone: The Collapse and Revival of American Community

Can we build a genuine community online with the people who frequent our blog, forum or social media platform? Before we explore this, let's clarify our intention for building a community.

If our intention is to create a pool of potential clients, we're not talking about community building - we're talking about marketing. This sales approach has a name; "community marketing". That's not what *we* mean by community. If marketing is the prime motivation for building community, it isn't a community we're talking about at all; it's a customer base.

When we attempt to build community on a blog, forum or social media platform, as opposed to building community on a video Hangout or in an offline setting, we face a challenge that we don't usually face offline: The people don't all gather at the same time. On a blog, for instance, people will drop by throughout the day the post is published and continue to drop by hours and even days, weeks and months later. Because of this, there is a lack of collaboration among the members. Typically, the interaction is between the author/leader and the rest.

The question then is this; can we build a community in an online space with all pillars in place? To answer this question, let's explore what we know about leading a group into community.

We know we start by creating the environment for the community to grow and by introducing the concept of community. We have to be busy hosting the meetings and moderating a discussion, and in the process, looking out for the community. But that's just the start.

Once the people have gathered, and interactions begin, we can observe our group and identify where we are in the community building process. Are we in pseudocommunity: Is everyone being excessively polite, biting back authentic opinions out of a fear of offending someone who holds a different one? Have we ventured into chaos: Have we had disagreements that made it feel as if the group were falling apart? Have we spent time in emptiness?

If the group is moving through the stages of the community building process, we can use the seven pillars as a checklist to gauge to what degree we are, or are becoming a community. Are the members committed to the group? Is it an inclusive group? Is the leadership shared among the members? Are the people authentic? And finally, is there a feeling of camaraderie and support?

If we have six of the seven pillars in place, we need to address the pillar of collaboration that is challenged by the fact that not everyone is present at the same time.

Encouraging interaction among the members, even if they are not all present at the same time, may successfully mitigate this. We live in an era of time-shifted communication. Not every email or chat message demands an immediate response. We can put an email, text, or chat message aside when we are busy and answer when we have the time. How nice to know we can show up at a blog or a forum or website hours after the bulk of the conversation has transpired, and someone may still be there to interact with, or to know we can leave a message and someone will reply later.

How does a blog look when it is a community? In the heyday of the Blogosphere, many said my blog, lifeforinstance.com [LFI], was a community. Time-travel with me to 2011 to see what you think.

I started LFI to create a place for people to talk about life. I love the idea of a front porch where you can sit with friends and sip tea or coffee and "solve all the problems of the world", so I referred to LFI as a porch. I made the page warm and inviting and welcomed everyone who came by. In this way, I set the tone for my blog. (I created the environment where community could grow.)

I talked often about community; I responded to every comment. (I introduced the concept of community.)

I moderated the discussion by finding topics that would stir debate and by having guest authors do the same. I referred comments to members I felt would have answers when I didn't have them or when I felt someone else could respond better than I could, encouraging collaboration. (I encouraged communication among the members.)

Then I spent a lot of time there, on the LFI porch, watching to see what would happen. (I waited)

In time, I noticed that the people were not just interacting with me but with one another, and I felt that camaraderie was developing among us. We collaborated on the big issues of life. We were an inclusive group. We became a safe harbour, a place where people entrusted us with their fears and frustrations. Even today, people who happen upon the blog say they feel welcome there, safe, and supported, and that, on the LFI porch, they feel at home.

However, we did not experience chaos or emptiness as a group, so it may be said that we partied in pseudocommunity. I'm pretty sure I said it wasn't that easy to build community, but in a non-synchronous setting such as a blog, forum or social media site, the challenges are much greater.

The Turn of the Tide

"For the first two-thirds of the twentieth century
a powerful tide bore Americans
into ever deeper engagement
in the life of their communities,
but a few decades ago
- silently, and without warning -
that tide reversed
and we were overtaken by a treacherous rip current...
over the last third of the century."
~ Robert D. Putnam
Bowling Alone: The Collapse and Revival of American Community

Just as the tide turned in the 1960's when people began to move away from social connectedness, now, at the beginning of the twenty-first century, the tide is turning again. The popularity of social media is telling us this: It is evidence of the turn of the tide.

Social media regularly presents examples of people reaching out to others; the homeless, the hungry, the oppressed, the forgotten. Messages of injustice -- and what we can do about it-- go viral. Twitter, Instagram, and Facebook have become forums for discussion on racism, misogyny, feminism, politics and more. Photos and videos of random acts of kindness receive millions of shares on Facebook. Celebrities and non-celebrities alike take up causes and share them via social media. It was social media that empowered Arab Spring and the Occupy movement.

Social media is facilitating connection among the citizens of earth like nothing that has come before.

Summary

Digitally enabled communication represents hope; we can't build community with people unless we can connect with them. Technology offers us a way to connect from the comfort of our homes and offices, porches and backyard swings, with people in all parts of the world in a way never before possible. This is important. As Putnam says, *"...it is hard to imagine solving our contemporary civic dilemmas without computer-mediated communication."*

There is an unprecedented opportunity here for you and me. As a human species, we are at the precipice of either extinction or evolution beyond our wildest imaginings, and the means to drive positive change through the power of community is at our fingertips. So where do we begin? We begin with the children.

10

Raising Community Builders

"I believe that if we are to survive as a planet,
we must teach this next generation
to handle their own conflicts assertively and non-violently.
If, in their early years,
our children learn to listen to all sides of the story,
use their heads and then their mouths,
and come up with a plan and share,
then, when they become our leaders,
and some of them will,
they will have the tools
to handle global problems and conflict."
~Barbara Coloroso
Kids Are Worth it: Giving Your Child The Gift Of Inner Discipline

Is there anything in life more important than the responsibility of parenting? It's up to us to ensure that the children of today are happy, wholesome, confident, competent, responsible, balanced, and resourceful individuals. It is essential that we give them three crucial messages for the journey of their lives: you are loved, you are not alone, and we are all in this together. These are the three promises of community.

How do we convey these messages to our children? We give them the experience of being a part of a community. This teaches our children about the importance of being inclusive and open to differing opinions and it exposes them to a model of mutual respect, collaboration, consensus, sharing of leadership, honest and authentic communication, and support for the people in their lives. These are not only values we want our children to embrace; they are values we want our leaders to possess.

Just as we pass on our values of generosity, kindness, and integrity to our children, we teach them about the importance of community. We do it at every opportunity and at every level of their development.

The First Community

"...We need to prepare them to join with others,
so they'll be capable of becoming a part of a "we".
After all, just because the mind is equipped and designed
to connect with others
doesn't mean that a child
is born with relationship skills."
~Daniel J Siegel and Tina Payne Bryson
The Whole-Brain Child:
12 Revolutionary Strategies to Nurture Your Child's Developing Mind

Community building begins in the family. Children's first encounter with community is within this, their first significant group. If a child experiences community within his or her family, community will be what is familiar, and we always seek the familiar.

Children absorb the values of their parents: If we are excited about community, our children will be too. If we are community builders, our children will have the opportunity to learn about the value of community by observation and participation. If we see the world through the lenses of community, our children, too, will come to see the world in this way.

As soon as we can, we introduce community to our children. We explain that we are a community, a special team. We talk about how we take care of one another. We work together, each doing the part we take care of one another. We work together, each doing the part he or she can do: Parents, we explain, contribute financial support, food purchasing and preparation, house maintenance, and other tasks the children are too young for yet; children contribute by picking up their toys and helping with household chores at age-appropriate levels. We are respectful of one another and the environment in the home. This loving interaction creates a place of mutual respect, a place where everyone feels valued.

We begin to speak about community when the children are very young and as they grow, we add layers to our explanation. We point out that our family community can only exist because in the larger community, the community of our city or town, there are people who grow our food, provide our electricity, make our clothes and manage our cities and towns. We explain that every role from Maintenance Engineer to Mayor is important to the community. We show how our community extends much farther than the boundaries of our city or town by explaining that cities and towns are part of provinces or states and those are part of a country, a continent, and of the planet. Just as we don't leave toys around the home for others to trip over or pick up for us, we don't litter the city, and we don't pollute the lakes, and we don't destroy the environment. We teach our children to think as members of a community, fostering the community mindset that we are all in this together.

As we build community with our family, we need to guard against the tendency to build an insular community, one that can become exclusive. We include the extended family in our community, as well as close friends and neighbours. In multi-generation communities, there is always an elder to lend perspective to a situation ("This is not the end of the world."). And there is always a young person to introduce new technological advances to the family (It's a whole new world!") In an extended family and in multi-generational communities, there is always someone there for the children.

Our children watch us and take their cues from us. If we are inclusive, they will be too. Inclusivity, the most challenging pillar of community, needs to be a part of a child's first community.

Siegel and Payne, authors of *The Whole Brain Child,* explain that learning involves integrating both the left and the right brain. First, a child has an experience which impacts the right-brain (emotion), and then we help them to engage the left-brain by talking about it (logic, understanding) so they can process this experience. Adding language to experience integrates the knowledge in our brains. This is how we learn. We need to give our children the experience of community and then help them to process what they are experiencing.

Like adults, children learn best through hands-on experience. *"...'Playful parenting' is one of the best ways to prepare your children for relationships and encourage them to connect with others"*, say Siegel and Payne. Play is an excellent way to introduce children to the concept of community.

The Seven Pillars
of the Community-Building Parent

The seven pillars of community serve as a template for the community-building parent. During our daily interactions with our children, we not only introduce them to an experience of community, we find creative ways to give them a vocabulary to speak about it.

Commitment

"I love you and I care very deeply about everything that involves you."

Our children intuitively sense our level of commitment to them. It is essential that we are aware of the importance of our role as parents and that we have clear goals for parenting. We must be dedicated and passionate about parenting, willing to give it all we have to give and to ask family and friends for support when we need it. Our ideas about the best parenting practices are ever evolving so, like a doctor keeping up with current published studies, we stay up to date by gathering new information as it becomes available. We remain committed to being a worthy leader or co-leader of the team of our family.

Inclusivity

"I am here for you. If I have to be away for a little while, I will stay in touch while I am away."

As much as possible, especially when they are very young, we should take our children with us wherever we go. We need to be attentive to them and spend this precious time in the presence of our children so they will know they are a valuable part of our lives. The attachment bond between parents and child is crucial at this stage of life. In his book *Reaching Through Resistance*, Abbass says, *"A child who grows up with this uninterrupted parental bond will be able to relate to others without undue fear, anxiety, or defensiveness."*

Shared Leadership

*"What do **you** think? What ideas do you have?"*

As our children grow we need to give them the opportunity to experience leadership. We ask for their opinions, listen to them, and respect the little leaders-in-the-making. We teach the children that their thoughts and ideas are important and that they have something to contribute to the team.

Collaboration

"Let's put our heads together and see what we can come up with."

We teach children how to collaborate at an early age. We can collaborate with them on what colour pyjamas they should wear to bed, on which vegetables to eat first, on what gift to purchase or make or on what activity to do next. We show our children that we respect and value them by listening and empathizing. We make collaborating a game; the way we solve problems together.

Camaraderie

"I love spending time with you!"

Camaraderie comes from time spent having fun together. We need to plan activities and do them together. When my children were small, I liked to turn the lessons and chores into games. My daughter still remembers the "Sock Game" in which the winner was the one who matched the greatest number of clean socks from the laundry basket.

Authenticity

"I'm feeling a little sad (or angry, or tired) right now. I need a little time alone and then we can talk."

It is so important that we are authentic with our children. If we are upset, we shouldn't hide it from them. They sense it anyway, and our denying what they sense only confuses them. We teach our children that sometimes each of us, even mothers and fathers, get angry or become sad, but that everything will be okay.

Talking about our feelings is an opportunity to teach our children how to deal with distress, and to begin to pass on skills of problem-solving. If we let them see that we are vulnerable human beings, they will know it is okay to admit to having fear and insecurity. If we offer empathetic listening when they share their problems, they will feel safe in sharing their problems with us and we can help them to learn to deal with their feelings.

Support

"I've got your back. I believe in you."

This gives our children confidence. Knowing your family has your back is of inestimable value to *all* of us.

More Community Building Vocabulary

1. *"We are important to one another; we keep our word."* [Commitment]
2. *"We don't leave anyone out; everyone can play with us."* [Inclusivity]
3. *"We take turns leading; at times, you will be the leader."* [Shared Leadership]
4. *"We work together; we make sure everyone is okay with our decision."* [Collaboration via consensus]
5. *"We have fun together."* [Camaraderie]
6. *"We always tell the truth about how we feel; no one is going to tell you it's wrong to feel what you do."* [Authenticity]
7. *"We are here for one another."* [Support]

We point out these pillars as we interact in daily life. *"Look! We are taking turns being the leader! This is what a **community** does!"* Paying attention is crucial. We need to notice and seize opportunities to convey to our children the importance of community. If it is important to us, and if we convey this when they are very young, it will become important to them.

When we use these pillars as our guide during the early years of our children's lives, we provide a safe, inclusive, loving home base to them and foster in them a disposition that prepares them for community. By our loving attention to this vocation, we give our children the valuable experience of belonging to a community at home, their first community, before they go out into the world.

Community Building and Sports

"Onward we march together,
faithful may we ever be..."

~Line from my High School song

Today, parents enroll their children in organized sports at an early age. Team sports offer an excellent opportunity for community building but whether the opportunity is realized depends on the coach. Mr. Edwards, my Cross Country coach, had an intuitive sense of community. He not only encouraged in us an awareness of ourselves as a team, he stepped back to allow us to run with this idea. He didn't tell us to spread out along the course during the meets to cheer one another on. He didn't instruct us to psych one another up as we walked the course before the race. He didn't encourage us to pace a runner who was getting tired. He didn't have to. Children in sports who have coaches like Mr. Edwards will come to know that team spirit is more important than winning.

If we value community, we will interview the coaches before we enrol our children, to make sure they place as much onus on team building as they do on winning.

Be a Team Builder

When our children are small, opportunities for community building abound. Family celebrations, vacations, outings and parties, and other situations where people have to work together toward a common goal provide perfect opportunities for community building. These are situations that require planning and where conflict can arise; factors that give us the chance to deal with chaos and to play with consensus.

When my daughter's boyfriend and my niece joined our family for our summer vacation at our cottage, I said that everyone should plan a meal they would like to prepare and I would purchase the ingredients. On their assigned cooking day, they would be the "Chef" and they would be assisted by the "Sous Chef" they had chosen. The others would clean up after the meal. This arrangement ensured that no one was an outsider because everyone had a role to play. Every person felt as if he or she belonged.

I once heard that if you have books around your home, your children would be more apt to become readers. But we can do better than that. We can read to our children; we can take them to the library and help them check out books and we can let them see us settling in to enjoy a good book. If we want to inspire children to be community builders, we have to give them an experience of belonging to a community. Children learn to become community builders, when in their homes, community is the norm.

Collaborative Problem Solving

"... you'll need an open mind...
along with some patience (with yourself and your child)
as you're practicing new ways of interacting
and solving problems together."
~Ross W. Greene PhD
The Explosive Child: A New Approach for Understanding and Parenting
Easily Frustrated, Chronically Inflexible Children

In the book, *The Explosive Child,* Ross W. Greene introduces something he calls a Collaborative Problem Solving process. This system is brilliant. I highly recommend this book, especially if your child is "easily frustrated", because it teaches a communication method that parents can introduce to their children at an early age, a method that involves consensus.

Greene outlines three parenting styles - Plan A is an authoritative one ("It is because I say it is."), and Plan C is a laissez-faire style ("Do whatever you like.") In Plan B, the parent adopts a process that not only approaches problems collaboratively but also works on good communication with the child, which improves the relationship between parent and child by letting the child know that his or her thoughts and feelings matter.

Teaching Consensus to Children

"Consensus doesn't necessarily mean complete agreement.
*It just means that everyone **consents;***
they're willing to go along with it
for the sake of keeping the game going."
~Peter Gray
Free to Learn: Why Unleashing the Instinct to Play Will Make Our Children,
Happier,
More Self-Reliant, and Better Students for Life

When Natasha and Alex were young, our backyard was the place where the neighbourhood children congregated to play. Nearly daily, through my kitchen window, I heard them arguing over which game to play. My son, often the only boy among them, usually lost the arguments as the girls outnumbered him. Regularly these disputes resulted in the angry departure of one little girl who was displeased when she didn't get her way.

Intrigued with the idea of consensus, one day when I heard them arguing I decided to discover if a group of young children could grasp the concept. I went out to the back steps, called them over and sat them all down. *"We're going to play a **new** game,"* I said, *"It's called **Consensus!**"* I had captured their attention.

I picked up a toy drumstick lying on the landing and introduced it as the "Talking Stick". I said that only the person who was holding the talking stick could talk. No one else could speak unless the person holding the stick gave them permission to ask a question. One by one they would have a chance to hold the stick and share how they felt.

I stressed the importance of listening when someone was talking, saying, *"You have to listen so well that you can ask a question!"*

I told them that no one was allowed to leave until everyone was happy with the decision made by the group.

These were the only instructions I gave them before I left them on the steps to play the game. It proved to be enough. The children were under eight years old, yet they mastered consensus. After that, whenever there was a dispute, I would hear one child's voice ring out, *"We have to play Consensus!"* followed by the footfall of several children running up the steps.

Consensus is not just a game for children - it's the way a community makes decisions. It involves presenting the issue and allowing everyone to share their thoughts on it until the group arrives at an outcome that everyone consents to. There are guidelines for using consensus in the Appendix.

Community Building and Empathy

"All too often, when children or youth
are made to feel that they don't belong
their response is a desire to "get even".
The headlines capture
the most dramatic examples
of youth "getting even"
in the statistics of suicide, aggression
and murder."
~Mary Gordon
The Roots of Empathy: Changing the World Child by Child

Community is marked by a profound sense of empathy with others. Mary Gordon says, *"The ability to take the perspective of another person, to identify commonalities through our shared feelings is the best peace pill we have."* Where community has grown, empathy is present. The gift of empathy is that someone hears you without attempting to rescue you from your problems, conveying the message that you are loved, you will work it out, and you are not alone.

Children need to be listened to and to feel that someone understands them. This is the attention that makes them *feel* loved. When I was growing up, I knew my mother would always be there to listen to me as I worked out the conundrums of life. No matter what happened, I could pour it all out to her, and she would help me to deal with it.

Many children today leave school to return to an empty house or go to a Daycare facility to stay until their parents pick them up after work. As the number of children in a Daycare is greater than the number of caregivers, the children may not find anyone to listen to the problems they may need to share. Imagine what would happen if Daycare caregivers built genuine community there, if children had an entire group of people ready and willing to listen to them.

The Shared Meal

The shared meal offers an excellent opportunity for community building. Yet, in recent years, enjoying a meal together as a family has become the exception rather than the rule. This is a shame because mealtimes are a time when children can process their day in the presence of adults who care about them. It was at suppertime one day that we learned my son Alex was having a problem at school.

He was in middle school, and he had a nice group of friends. Recently, a boy who was not in their circle of friends had decided he wanted to sit with them in the lunchroom, but the seats at the table where the group sat were all occupied. Rather than pulling up a chair and squeezing in, the boy decided someone should leave to make room for him. He targeted Alex for this. When Alex would arrive at the table, the boy would say in a loud voice, *"Go away! We don't want you here!"*

As Alex shared the story, his father, sister and I could see how much this was upsetting him. We offered empathy, questions and suggestions. Alex went away and gave it some thought. The next day at suppertime, he told us what he had decided and what had resulted from his actions.

*He took his lunch to the table and when he arrived the boy said, "Go away. We don't want you here!" Alex stood his ground. He looked around the table at his friends and said, "**Who** doesn't want me here? Show of hands!" Not one child raised his hand. He then turned and looked at the boy, who puffed himself up, glared at Alex for a few seconds and then decided to find another place to sit.*

Neither his sister nor his father nor I had given him this solution; he came up with it on his own. We all have answers within us, wisdom we can access when someone who believes in us cares enough to listen.

My daughter, Natasha, had an opportunity to witness the power of empathy one summer day when she was organizing a game for a group of children. During the game, one child ran off to the side, visibly upset. Natasha paused the game and went over to him. She squatted down to be at his level and listened to him. After a few minutes, the child gave her a hug and happily ran back to join the game. Natasha was amazed; she had not solved any problems nor had she given any advice. She had only offered empathy.

Summary

Community can take root in our world today when we apply energy to the important task of fostering of the community mindset in our children. Just one person (you!) can be the instrument of profound change, by changing the world of a child - or perhaps, of a classroom of children.

11

Community Building in School

The Roots of Empathy

*"Every human being
has a deep need to be heard,
to be seen,
to belong"*
~ Mary Gordon
The Roots of Empathy: Changing the World Child by Child

Mary Gordon's *Roots of Empathy* program fosters the growth of empathy in children. In Gordon's words, *"It is a program that can instil in our children a concept of themselves as strong and caring individuals, to give them an understanding of empathic parenting and to inspire in them a vision of citizenship that can change the world."*

In the *Roots of Empathy* program, a mother and her infant visit a classroom once a week for nine months. The children are guided in their observation of the baby and the interaction between the baby and mother. Through this comprehensive curriculum, which continues during the weeks before and after the weeks of the baby's visit, the children learn to identify and name emotions. They learn that we all have fear and insecurity and the wide range of emotions they encounter in the program. The children go from having empathy for the baby to turning that empathy toward themselves to having empathy toward their classmates.

Children are capable of learning to be empathetic at a very young age. If the attachment bond between infant and parent is healthy, if the parent is lovingly responsive to the baby's needs, empathy can grow. But when this attachment bond is interrupted by death or separation caused by illness or neglect, there is a damaging effect on children. The *Roots of Empathy* program helps to alter the trajectory set in place in infancy for children who have not had a good start in life by setting them on a path which brings them to empathy and into community with their classmates, the teacher, and the instructor of the program. In the *Roots of Empathy* program, the children find a safe place to share their feelings, an inclusive place where diversities are accepted and celebrated, a fully interactive environment where everyone's gifts are recognized. Sound familiar?

Watch YouTube videos that introduce the *Roots of Empathy* program and you (like me) will be entranced. The *Roots of Empathy* program has spread to schools in countries all around the world. Bravo Mary Gordon - well, well done!

Even as we are still acquiring the skills of community building, we can offer empathy to the children we encounter in our lives. It's as simple as listening with attentive, loving ears; giving the children the message that someone sees them and cares about them, that their feelings are important, that they are not alone.

The Importance of Free Play

*"The decline of children's free play time
since about 1955
has been accompanied by a continuous rise
in anxiety, depression, and feelings of helplessness
in young people."*
~Peter Gray

Free to Learn: Why Unleashing the Instinct to Play Will Make Our Children Happier,
More Self-Reliant, and Better Students for Life

In *Free to Learn*, Peter Gray writes, *"Play is nature's way of teaching children how to solve their own problems, control their impulses, modulate their emotions, see from others' perspectives, negotiate differences, and get along with others as equals. There is no substitute for play as a means of learning these skills. They can't be taught in school."*

Play prepares children for community building. The playgrounds in the schoolyard and in our neighbourhoods are where we learn to come into community with others.

The Community Building Teacher

The school setting offers many group experiences that can become community building experiences for children; clubs, societies, team sports, student government and of course the classroom.

When I was in the ninth grade, I had a seat on Student Council. The advisor for Student Council introduced us to Beauchesne's Parliamentary Rules and Forms used in the Canadian House of Commons, a procedure that we followed at our meetings. Thanks to the guidance of this teacher, we had a glimpse into the workings of parliament. My twelfth-grade Political Science teacher taught us how to play "Caucus" to experience what happens in the House of Commons when representatives of different regions came together to push for their aims.

Imagine if all committee advisors and teachers led their groups in *community building* exercises! Every teacher standing before a group of children is in a position to introduce them to the magic of community.

Summary

We teach children to be community builders by modeling it, valuing it, focusing on it, explaining it and providing a vocabulary for it. We identify it and the absence of it, we make it the way our "team" operates in the world. We don't leave anyone out.

Imagine if, as a child, you went from a community at home to a community at school and later to a community at daycare or a team sports arena before returning to your home community at the end of the day. Having *just one* significant community in our lives can make all the difference to us. Imagine what a powerful impact having this many communities can have on the lives of our children.

If we are to charge our children with the task of solving the problems we're leaving to them, isn't it only right that we provide them with tools for solving them? Through the fostering of community building with our children, we will be impressing upon them the importance of inclusivity, camaraderie, openness to differing opinions, mutual respect, collaboration, consensus, sharing of leadership, honesty, authentic communication and mutual support. These are the ideas we want our future leaders to embrace.

It is our most important task to teach the children about community. To do that, we need to become familiar with it ourselves. Through our actions, we will create a world in which no one will be discriminated against because of race or economics, sex or sexual orientation, age, culture or religion. No one will be put down, excluded or ignored. Political decisions will be made by consensus and the political machine, itself a community, will make decisions that are good for everyone without harming the planet. All will be invited to the table of discussion. These children, the ones we introduce to community today, will foster a spirit of collaboration, camaraderie, fellowship and peace.

In the world today, there are at least 31 different forms of government. All involve a system of hierarchy. Children who have been raised to be community builders will not accept hierarchy. They will have experienced the power of the circle.

Listen! Can you hear the sound of the drums?

12

Seeing the World Through the Lens of Community

Our Global Evolution

*"You can change the world
if you're prepared to imagine something better."*
~Edward Rutherfurd
New York: the novel

We are not the people we were just a century ago. Our attitudes are changing and because of this, our behaviour is changing too. We are changing the way we parent our children thanks to a greater understanding of child psychology and we are making efforts to create a better education system. We are changing the way we treat ethnic minorities, the poor, the elderly, women, LBGTQ individuals, immigrants, people of different religions, the physically challenged, the mentally ill. We are changing the way we treat the most vulnerable among us.

Just a century ago, it was as unthinkable to divorce one's spouse even if there was physical abuse, and society frowned upon two people living together before they were married. Just fifty years ago, we believed we had to control the will of our children, and some believed, our spouse, with violence if necessary. Fifty years ago, the mentally challenged and the mentally ill were routinely institutionalized, not welcome in society.

We maintained appearances at all costs, and the cost was high. Our attitudes and actions were based on an old belief system, one that we were only beginning to question. The world was not a kinder gentler place; it only appeared that way from the outside, and only when we were looking through the windows of the homes of the privileged.

We followed the rules. We never "aired our dirty laundry in public", we obeyed church decrees without questioning them. We maintained the facade that all was well. We were in **pseudocommunity**...

Then someone said, *"Wait a minute!"* At last.

"Why shouldn't a woman be able to vote?" "Why should I ride at the back of the bus?" "Why do we treat homosexuals and transsexuals so badly?" More questions arose. "Why are we hitting our children?" "Why should a woman make less than the man who does the same job that she does?" We said it was wrong to discriminate against people for their race or religion. We questioned the supremacy of church and state. We began to question-- everything.

And this questioning brought us into **chaos...**

Gradually, more people found the courage to speak out. They took up the battle for equality among the races and the sexes, for nuclear disarmament, for an end to war and the destruction of our environment. Because of the actions of these brave souls, we saw painfully gained, inch-by-inch forward motion in our evolution.

It's just begun but the signs are everywhere. Hierarchies are beginning to crumble. The top-down method of management, of governing, of running our businesses, of leading the religious flocks, are failing. Democracy, while better than most other systems of governing, is not the best we can do. The shape of our hope is not a pyramid. It's a circle. We are in chaos, a precarious, scary place, yet a state preferable to one in which we pretended that everything was fine, a state in which so many suffered in silence. Now, those who had been silenced are speaking out with one voice. We have a long, long way to go, but we have begun the march.

We are approaching the next stage on our global journey, **emptiness...**

We will never find answers when we believe we already have them. We will never question our judgments until we recognize that they are judgments. In the past, we ignored the problems or fought about them unproductively, but the answers are never found hiding in the dark, or in the noise of the fight but in the silence that settles over us when the battle has ended.

Analyzing our opinions and relinquishing our judgments will not be easy; we will not easily let go of the desire for control. We will not willingly surrender the trappings of the familiar, but much of what was considered normal not that long ago is no longer accepted by the enlightened minds that shine the light of reason upon it.

We can't solve a problem until we recognize that there is a problem. Pseudocommunity hid the problems. It divided us, so that we did not gather to discuss the problems. Chaos arose when we began to take a good hard look at our problems. As much as we dislike chaos, trading chaos for emptiness will come with a feeling of great fear. But emptiness is where we find the solutions to the problems that chaos has revealed.

We may not walk willingly into emptiness, but one thing is clear; *we won't go back to pseudocommunity.*

We need to empty ourselves of our judgments and question and evaluate what we once accepted as true. We must discard our acceptance of division, the belief in the value of hierarchies, the status quo in which few have wealth and power while everyone else struggles to make a living. Emptiness is the way out of this chaos: There is no other way.

We are all human beings who share this planet. We are all concerned about the futures of our children, about the sustainability of the place we call home. It's time we worked together to solve our problems.

The tide is slowly rising and a high tide, as they say, raises all boats. In his book, *Memoirs*, Pierre Elliott Trudeau talked about the peace initiative he took at the end of his time in the office of the Prime Minister of Canada. He wrote, *"In that dreadful fall of 1983, the government of Canada was the first to realize the necessity for speaking out. The sceptics were wrong. Our ideas of hope for an end to the Cold War carried more weight than their fears."*

Nothing will stop this rising tide. We have battled nature to survive; we have waged war on one another both for territory and for power; we have fought for our rights--for equality and personal freedoms, and now we are struggling to hold onto those freedoms, which are being threatened by efforts to keep us safe.

We need a new mindset, one that recognizes that we are all in this together. We need a **community** mindset.

When we come into community globally, the resources now allocated to the war effort and security will be redirected to support the people of this planet. An organism that is in flight or fight mode has little energy left for maintenance and repair. When we invoke the relaxation response, globally, healing will take place on a global level. Then we will be communities uniting with communities rather than countries fighting for power. We'll stop killing people and begin to feed them; we'll stop building weapons of destruction and instead collaborate to create and build clean energy systems to support the planet. We will witness the richness of other cultures, and other cultures will observe ours, and no one will have to change who they are to gain acceptance by the others.

What will happen to loneliness, aggression, suicide and crimes of violence and terrorism when we begin to cooperate socially, when everyone is a part of the community? Can there be any doubt that our next evolutionary leap will be one into community?

We live in an age that presents tremendous challenges and yet offers opportunities as no other times have before. It is a time of hope. If enough people hold the vision of community in their minds and hearts, we will eventually reach a critical mass, and then together, we will change everything. When we recognize that we are *all* "we"-- that there is nobody else here but us -- there can be only peace.

Cohousing

*"Pocket neighborhoods can help mend
the web of belonging, care,
and support needed
in a frayed world."*
~ Ross Chapin
*Pocket Neighborhoods;
Creating Small-scale Community in a Large-scale World*

In Denmark in the nineteen-sixties, a Danish architect, Jan Gudmand-Hoyer, conceived of a cooperative living model, a multi-unit complex where people could live together in community. He called it *bofaellesskab* (living community). Later, two American authors dubbed the concept "cohousing".

Cohousing complexes have small individual units positioned around a "common house" that has a large kitchen, living room, recreation room, laundry facilities and other amenities. The parking area is at the perimeter of the compound so that the interior, common area (usually with a green space) is a safe place for children to play, and serves to facilitate daily interaction among residents. While the families living in cohousing complexes have private living spaces, they come together to share meals and to enjoy and support one another.

Architect Ross Chapin called this community-facilitating living arrangement "pocket neighbourhoods." In his book, he introduces many variations of pocket neighbourhoods; both built by design and created by altering an existing area by removing backyard fences or by reclaiming and greening a backyard alley to connect the homes on either side.

Cohousing and pocket neighbourhoods provide a viable, friendly contrast to apartment living. This concept is catching on. Pocket neighbourhoods and cohousing complexes are springing up in the US, Canada, Australia, New Zealand, Japan and the United Kingdom, and the movement is growing.

The world is marching toward community.

Community Rising Like the Phoenix

November 14, 2015. I was up late last night watching the heartbreaking news out of Paris following the coordinated attacks on innocent civilians; assaults that took at least 120 lives and left many other young people injured and in critical condition. The following morning, in the aftermath of that horrible tragedy, this book about community building and hope seems idealistic and inadequate. I wonder if it is too late; if we've gone too far, if the chaos will ever give way to emptiness.

I don't have any answers, and I don't know what to do about that. Oh, but I *want* to know what to do about it. How do we eliminate narrow-mindedness or give sight back to the blind? How do we heal generations of revenge seeking and hatred, crippling poverty, greed and the destruction caused by the relentless pursuit of power?

In 1964, when Martin Luther King Jr. accepted his Nobel Peace Prize he said:

> *"...I refuse to accept the view that mankind is so tragically bound to the starless midnight of racism and war that the bright daybreak of peace and brotherhood can never become a reality..."*

Unless you knew who said this, you would believe it was said today.

But I'm not a quitter, and I live in a world of people who, like me, refuse to quit. You see, community rises like the Phoenix from the ashes in situations like these. The evidence is indisputable; from the messages on Twitter - *#PorteOuverte* [open door] - where citizens of Paris offered a safe haven to strangers stranded in the city because of the closed transit system, to the taxi drivers who turned off their lights and drove people home free of charge, to the singing of the national anthem by the frightened people as they were vacating the stadium, to the long line-ups the following morning of people waiting to donate blood for the wounded lying in hospitals; a brotherhood survives. Fellowship and concern for one's fellow man and woman will always triumph because, evidently, even horrible acts like these can't snuff out *this* candle.

Community remains the uncrushable force.

It's Possible

"No matter how much you differ with someone on the surface,
the deeper you go, the more you'll find in common.
Do the work, spend the time,
care enough to create deep connections,
and get great things done."
~ Ralph Marston

In the wee hours of the morning of November 9th, 2016, after an unusually hostile election campaign, Donald J Trump was elected the 45th president of the United States. Still lying in bed that morning, I reached for my iPod to learn of the election results. I discovered I'd just missed a long and anxious, conversation in a group chat among three members of my Hangout community; James in India, Stu in the US and Rose who heard the news while travelling in Australia. By the time I got there, they were all offline but now I knew who had won the election.

Like many that morning, I got up and turned on the television and opened my laptop, tuning into traditional media and social media simultaneously. I read and listened for most of that day and night.

I observed that the politicians in all parties immediately dropped their campaign rhetoric of division and competition and began talking about healing the wound of division that the election had inflicted on the population. This is an action that needs to be taken in the aftermath of *every* election, but I doubt that it was ever needed more than it was needed now.

Then it struck me.

If, after months of pre-election fighting and acrimony, we could come together to repair the damage, why couldn't we come together *in the first place?* If we can reconcile after such an energy-charged and obscenely expensive campaign, why couldn't we instead apply all that energy, time and money to the goal of building a diverse, effective, well-oiled, genuine community to lead our countries?

Our electoral system itself is divisive. Imagine charging a group of the brightest children on the planet with the task of dividing themselves into two or more groups, fighting for nearly two years to discover who the winner will be, clean or dirty fighting - doesn't matter - and then instruct them to "heal the wound of division". It is a recipe for failure.

To say, "This is democracy" as if that is the best we can do, is to accept the unacceptable.

Is it possible that a large number of political representatives can build community; a place of mutual respect, support, authenticity, collaboration, camaraderie, inclusivity, commitment and shared leadership, a place where decisions are made by consensus?

There is a bigger question: Is it possible that we are not making the gravest of errors in allowing ourselves to be governed by a system that promotes to positions of power people-cum-politicians who aspire to less than this?

Start Communities

Scott Peck finished *The Different Drum* with two words: *"Start communities"*. I echo Peck's call to action with the sounding of my drum. All we need to do is begin. In our small beginnings, in the building of communities on a personal level, is the power to change the world.

When we build just one community, a few more people on the planet will feel less alone, and the ripples of joy of community will spread out around us. Global community is humanity's hope for survival, but we need only begin here, on a personal level: We can change the world by changing our world, the place where all things begin.

Let's build communities with our peers. Let's build communities with the children in our lives, with our students, our friends, our Bible study group, our co-workers, our sports teams. Let's build communities with our friends, with the members of our associations, with our fellow parishioners. Let's invite our children's teachers to our community building groups so they will know how to build communities at school with the other teachers. Then more teachers will be inspired to build communities in the classrooms and more children will experience community.

Let's become familiar with the *Roots of Empathy* program and do what we can to get it into our school systems. Let's beat the drum of community building by passing *this* book on to teachers and other leaders in our cities and towns.

What we begin today will reverberate into the future, one beat at a time.

Will You Sound Your Drum?

"Those who make peaceful revolution impossible will make violent revolution inevitable."
~ John F. Kennedy

Peaceful revolution must be our goal. Can you conceive of a world in which all people lived together in peace? We won't ever see it if we can't first imagine it.

Is it presumptuous to think that if we come into community globally, we will find the answers we need to survive peacefully on this planet? No, the opposite is true: It is ludicrous to believe we will find the answers if we *fail* to come into community.

The unification of all citizens on Team Earth will make war impossible. We can't turn our guns upon people who are "us". The real power to bring about world peace is contained in the awareness that we are **all** us and it comes to fruition with the building of community.

We have never needed community more than we need it today. Though we keep pace to the beat of our own drums we can--and must--march together. We must sound our drums in harmony, joy, and peace. Before it is too late.

It's time.

APPENDIX

Tools for Community Building

In this section:

1. Steps for setting up your social media platforms for community building.
2. Guidelines for using Consensus.
3. A Book Club community building exercise based on a study of this book.
4. Twenty-two "Community Building Conversation Starters"; sets of questions based on life themes that will lead your group in discussions to facilitate connections and lay the foundation for community building.
5. Five "Group-Specific Conversation Starters".
6. Community Building games.
7. Resource list of the wonderful books mentioned.

Setting up Your Social Media Platform

1. **Facebook** Finding people to build your community can be as simple as posting an invitation on Facebook to ask who is interested in having an experience of community building. As well, you can reach out by private message to people you know. If you don't have a Facebook here are some details to help you set up an account.

    a.   Go to www.facebook.com and follow instructions for setting up your account. If you want more help, GOOGLE *"YouTube: how use Facebook"*. Select a video with the most recent date as social media sites change frequently. Once you have set up your page, find your friends by typing their names in the Search field at the top (the one that says "Search Facebook") and clicking on the magnifying glass icon. When you find a friend, click "Add Friend." When you do this, they will receive a message that you want to be friends. They will need to accept your invitation to complete the process. Once you have a number of friends you would like to build community with, go to the next step.

b.   Beneath the words "Update Status" is an empty place to type with the words "What's on your mind?" or something to that effect. This field is where you put your "post", something your friends will see. Just type your invitation in there and then click "Post". People can reply to you there and you can respond to them.

c.   If you would like to send a private invitation to someone, type their name in the "Search Facebook" field. Then, when you get to their page, look for the word "Message". Clicking on Message will open a private chat box.

d.   Ask each person who responds positively to invite two or three friends. Once you have some individuals who want to join you, (five or six is a good start), you can create a private Facebook Group chat by opening a Message box and adding the members, one by one.

2) If you are planning to meet online, find a forum to use for your video chats; Skype, Google+ Hangout, or Facebook video chats. Technology is producing new offerings regularly. Try out different ones and use what works best. To learn how to use them, Google or YouTube your question. If you are planning to meet offline, find a cafe with a large table or plan to meet in your homes, rotating homes for each meeting.

3) Use the Private Chat to communicate with members and find a time and date for the first meeting.

Guidelines for Using Consensus

1. Adjust to group size. A small group may easily flow into the consensus process, with each person taking a turn to share his or her views. If the group is larger, you may like to use a Talking Stick, passing it around the circle, to stay aware of sharing the floor.

2. Be age-appropriate. For children, a colorful, feather-topped Talking Stick may be the best way to go. I say "feather-topped" because as you talk and wave the stick (those of us who talk with their hands), the feathers will move and catch the eye, helping the speaker be more aware of how much he or she is taking of the discussion time. This is a valuable tool for a group of adults for the same reason.

3. Discover different formats. Use the consensus guidelines you will find online by conducting a search online with these words: "How to do consensus." Search and experiment until you find one that suits your group.

4. Everyone is heard. Let each person be heard and even questioned to be sure everyone has understood them.

5. Hash it out. Discuss as a group the possible courses of action.

6. Don't quit. Continue the discussion until everyone is in harmony with the suggested action.

7. Remember, the goal is to come to a decision that everyone is willing to go along with.

Starting a Book Club with *Sounding the Drum*

This book is a great subject for a community building Book Club because when everyone reads the book, everyone has the tools, immediately casting all members in the role of leader, which puts less pressure on you. Here is a format for the meetings.

Meeting #1: Have everyone read Chapters 1 and 2. Use these questions to begin a discussion:

1. Have you ever been in a group that felt like a community? What brought you together, what caused the group to disband?
2. Did you ever live in a neighbourhood that felt like a community?
3. Describe an experience you had as a member of a team.
4. Do you have a group like this in your life now?
5. Do you think we can build community together here?

Meeting #2: Chapter 3

1. Have you ever connected with groups of people online?
2. What was the level of connection with these people? How close did you feel to them?
3. Are you in any Facebook groups or Forums with an authentic feeling of connection?
4. Have you ever felt connected to the citizens of your city/town in a significant way?

Meeting #3: Chapter 4

1. What would be your one-sentence definition of community?
2. Which of the pillars can you most relate to in a group you have been in?
3. Which pillar do you feel is the most important one and why?
4. Can you imagine a group in which all seven pillars are in place?

Meeting #5: Chapter 5 and 6

1. Can you relate to the stage of pseudocommunity in any group you are or have been in? How did it feel to be in this stage?
2. Did you ever see a group break up when it moved into chaos? Did you witness a group retreat to pseudocommunity?
3. Have you experienced the stage of emptiness?
4. What stage do you think this group is in right now?

Meeting #6: Chapter 7

1. Can you relate to the community-building path as it pertains to a friendship or a partnership that you are or have been in?
2. After reading the section on emotional healing, can you imagine that awareness of the community building path can help you work through an emotional issue?
3. Can you relate to these stages of grief?
4. Where do you think you are in the evolution through the stages in your life?
5. Did you apply the Relationship Checklist to your current or past relationships?

Meeting #7: Chapter 8

1. Do you have a group in your life where you can answer the question, "How are you?" with candid honesty?
2. Who is the main witness to your life?
3. What group in your life makes you feel less alone?
4. "Community can help our species to survive." Is this true?
5. Have you ever found yourself enjoying community vicariously through sitcoms or other television shows? Which shows speak of community to you?

Meeting #8: Chapter 9

1. Can the digital connection be authentic?
2. Technology: good or bad?
3. Do you agree: "The digital age adds another layer to the definition of "propinquity". Does this mean our online friends can be real friends?

4. Do you believe the world is turning more and more towards community?

Meeting #9: Chapter 10

1. Do you believe it is possible to introduce community to children at a young age?
2. How can we teach parents the language of community?
3. How can we influence coaches to be community builders for our children?
4. Have you ever "played" consensus? Can you imagine teaching this game to the children in your life?
5. Was the shared meal a standard practice when you were growing up? Was it a part of life when your children were young?

Meeting #10: Chapter 11

1. Were you inspired to watch a YouTube video of the *Roots of Empathy*, or to pick up the book when you read about it? What can we do to get this program into our schools?
2. Do you believe free playtime can improve our education system?
3. How can we inspire teachers in our schools to be community builders?

Meeting #11: Chapter 12

1. Which stage of the community building process do you believe we are in globally?
2. Do you believe we will make it to community?
3. What do you think of Cohousing and Pocket Neighbourhoods? Can you imagine living in one?
4. How relevant is political leadership in this movement?
5. Community rising like the phoenix: we watch, we feel, we are vicariously a part of the community, yes or no?
6. Name three political leaders, past or present, who are community builders and three who are not.
7. Politically, can we do better than the electoral systems now in place?
8. Will you build one community? Will you sound your drum?

Meetings 12 - and more, have fun with the Community Building Conversations. Have you built yourselves into a community? Will you take these skills and build community with other groups? Seriously, after moving through this community building process *you know how* to sound your drum.

Community Building Conversation Starters

Although we can encourage a group to evolve into community, the leader can't force a group to become a community. A community is something a group of people builds together. The leader's role is to encourage that growth by facilitating meaningful communication among the members.

We do not naturally move immediately from "how are you?" to revealing our deepest insecurities. The process is slower and more respectful of the boundaries we have erected over a lifetime of learning to protect ourselves from the sometimes-hurtful response to such sharing.

We guide the group in conversation with a gentle, gradual process. Our approach is much like our approach to a swim in a cold lake. We would feel shocked by a plunge off the end of a wharf; we prefer to slowly wade into the lake from the edge of the water. With this awareness, we guide the group in conversations that lead gradually from discussions at the "edge of the shore" to those in "deeper waters".

Note: in some ways, spontaneous community springs from a plunge off the end of a wharf into a cold lake, but this is because of the crisis, which inspires the run to the end of the wharf. We can't force a group into community. The organic community building process is much gentler and, lacking a crisis, more fun.

The objective of these conversations is to connect with one another through the sharing of our stories. Our stories are how we define ourselves. When we share our stories, we begin to admit people to our inner circle. Through the sharing of our stories, we make connections with one another. This is how community building progresses, one story at a time.

Sift through the different Community Building Conversations to find one that is right for your group. Following these twenty General Conversations are five Group Specific ones. You may find one there for your group, or you can use one as a template to create a set of questions for your group.

The General Conversation Starters

1) Introducing Community

1. Have you ever had a Best Friend Forever [BFF] with whom you felt you could share anything and be yourself? Tell us about this friendship.
2. Have you ever had a close friendship end because of a conflict? [Experience with chaos.]
3. Have you ever made a snap judgment about someone and then made a conscious decision to suspend that judgement and learn that you liked that person? [Choice to move to emptiness.]
4. Have you ever been a member of a group of people who started as strangers and became close? Tell us about it. [Community building.]
5. When and where in your life have you felt safe enough and free enough to be who you are? [Spirit of community.]
6. Have you ever been part of a meaningful community?
7. Do you know who you are and are you willing to explore that in an authentic community building experiment here?

2) Intense Community Building Session

1. Share something silly about yourself
2. Tell about the thing in your life that makes you happiest.
3. Finish this sentence; "My greatest desire is …"
4. Tell about the best gift anyone ever gave you.
5. Tell about something in your life that makes you sad.
6. What is your most troublesome worry?
7. Share something that nobody knows about you.

8. Finish this sentence, "In groups, I usually feel..."
9. Share one regret you wish you could erase from your life.
10. What is your greatest fear?
11. What is your greatest source of pride?
12. Finish this sentence, "deep inside I feel..."

3) The Pillars of Community

1. Have you ever been a part of a fully committed group of people working together towards a common goal? [Commitment]
2. Talk about a time when you were excluded from something you wanted to be a part of [Inclusivity]
3. Have you ever been a part of a group with a dynamic leadership, where everyone's gifts and skills were called upon? [Shared leadership]
4. Tell us about an experience with a group of people that was fully collaborative and successful [collaboration]
5. What was your most precious experience of camaraderie with a group of people? [Camaraderie]
6. Do you have a group of people with whom you can be your authentic self and not feel judged or afraid to be so? [Authenticity]
7. Who's got your back? [Support]

4) Who are you?

1. How would you describe yourself?
2. How did you become who you are? Were you born this way or did circumstances in your life create you or did you create yourself?
3. Do you like yourself? What do you like and what do you dislike about yourself?
4. Finish this sentence: If I could change one thing about myself it would be...

5) Your Path in Life

1. When you were a teenager, what did you see as your path in life ahead?
2. Did you ever want to follow one of your parent's career paths?
3. How did your plan change as you graduated from High School - and up to the present?
4. Did anyone give you the message, when you were young, that you needed to find a good income-producing career?
5. Did anyone guide you well, or not so well, in the choices you made?
6. Do you believe we have a pre-ordained path or that we tweak as we go and as we get to know ourselves?
7. Are you happy with where you are now and optimistic about the future?

6) What is Happiness?

1. On a scale of one to ten, how happy are you right this minute with 1 being not happy at all and 10 being ecstatically happy?
2. Are some people just born happier than others? What do you believe makes them so?
3. Do you think people have a happiness default, a mood they settle back into when they are not stimulated to feel something else? How can we change the default?
4. Do you think there are times in our lives when we are naturally happier, say in childhood, for instance, or does our happiness maintain the same level throughout life?
5. What is your best advice for happiness?
6. If you could go back in time and visit your five-year-old self or your nineteen-year-old self, what would you say about happiness?

7) Is Life Fair

1. What made you smile yesterday?
2. Do you consider yourself to be a fair person?
3. Do you believe a fair person such as yourself created you and all of your life?

4. Where do we get our sense of fairness?
5. Is life fair?

8) Authenticity

1. What was your most embarrassing moment?
2. What is the craziest thing you've ever done?
3. What is the most out-of-character thing you've ever done?
4. What is the most authentic thing you've ever done - the most in-character?
5. Do you feel happier when you are authentic? Share an example.

9) Laughter

1. What made you laugh recently?
2. What is your favourite type of humour?
3. What is the funniest joke you've ever heard?
4. Tell about a time when you laughed but you should not have laughed.
5. Tell about a joke you've told in perfect timing.
6. What sitcoms do you enjoy?
7. What are your favourite funny movies?

10) Good News: Bad News

1. Did you ever get up on the wrong side of the bed but the day got better and better?
2. Did you ever meet someone and think "Oh no!" but then your opinion of them changed?
3. Did something ever happen to you that felt like a calamity but then it turned out to be a blessing in disguise?
4. Do we have the power to turn things around?
5. Should we, and could we, never, ever judge anything?

11) Are You Fickle?

1. Did you ever begin something with excitement and then end up bored?
2. How long have you been in the same job/career?
3. Did you ever outgrow a friendship?
4. Are you fickle and is that a bad thing?
5. Have you ever had to accept change you didn't want to accept?
6. What bores you?

12) Perfection

1. What for you is a perfect hot beverage?
2. What is the perfect awakening moment?
3. What is/was your most perfect pet?
4. What was your most perfect vacation?
5. What is/was your most perfect friendship?
6. If perfection is in our minds, can we make or perceive something as perfect?

13) Messages from Movies

1. What was the first movie you recall seeing in a theatre? How did it affect you?
2. What was the first romantic movie you can remember seeing? What was its message to you?
3. What one-liners from movies have stuck in your mind?
4. What damaging or misleading messages do we receive from movies?
5. What was the best message you can remember receiving from a movie?

14) Thinking

1. What is your usual first thought upon awakening?
2. Do you pause to adjust your thinking when you awaken with a negative thought?
3. Have you ever seen a random thought manifest as something you wanted in your life?

4. Is your cup half full or half empty?
5. Would you say you spend more time thinking about the past, the present or the future?
6. Do you believe your thoughts create your life?
7. Do you think too much? Is it possible to think too much?
8. What thoughts describe the life you really want to live going forward?
9. What do you think about as you are falling asleep at night?

15) How Much Control Do We Have?

1. Name two things in your life that you control.
2. Tell about one thing you manifested recently.
3. Did you ever want something very badly and then you got it?
4. Have you ever looked back at a "bad' thing and realized it was a good thing after all?
5. Have you ever manifested a passing desire that you had only thought about once?
6. On a scale of one - ten, how much control do we have? Why?

16) Pre-Holiday Meeting: Wishes

1. What is one thing about the past year that makes you proud?
2. Tell about one thing in your life that makes you feel fiercely grateful.
3. What is one small thing you want to manifest in the next month?
4. What are three predominant feelings you would like to feel during the holidays?
5. What big thing will you manifest in the next 12 months?
6. What major thing in your life will have changed by this time next year?
7. What is your one wish for the world?

17) Post Holiday Meeting: Perfection

1. Describe one small perfect moment over the holidays.
2. Did your Holidays go the way you had hoped?

3. Did you ever look back on something as perfect when it didn't feel perfect as it was happening?
4. Who decides what is perfect?
5. Is it possible that our lives are perfect even at times when we don't think they are?

18) Controlling our Happiness

The quote that inspired this topic: Don said, "We are happiest when we are rolling with what happens in life."

1. Describe a time when you missed the moment because you judged what was going on and said it was not good.
2. If it is within our control to choose our perspective and our perspective determines our happiness, so how much control do we really have? i.e. Don rolls with what happens so is he happier than I am?
3. If we can control our happiness, then don't we have enough control because happiness is how we judge and why we want what we want. So, if we have what we want, doesn't that mean we have a lot of control?
4. What do we do about death, sickness, tragedy?
5. Jamie says it is the thrill of the ride that makes us want to get on a roller coaster but a roller coaster is not always up - it is down as much as it is up. What do you make of that?

19) What is Time?

1. Have you ever experienced time as flying by? When?
2. Do you have a place you like to go where it feels as if time does not exist?
3. Have you ever had the experience where time slowed down so you could accomplish something or be on time?
4. Have you ever had a dream that seemed to go on for hours but lasted only minutes?
5. What if time does not exist?

6. What if we knew that death and tragedy would be a part of life before we came to this life and we were okay with that because we knew time didn't exist?

20) Promises

1. Have you ever had a friend arrive late for a meeting - or a friend who is always late?
2. Is an appointment, or a date, a promise?
3. Is it a promise when you don't use the word "promise"?
4. Do you find you keep or break promises to yourself with the same frequency as you keep or break them with others?
5. Would you prefer a promise not be made at all rather than be made and broken?
6. Do we appreciate something someone does for us as much when it is merely the fulfillment of a promise or do we take that for granted?
7. Marriage vows are promises. Don't we need promises?
8. Do you make promises?
9. Did you ever break a promise?

21) Business --or Pleasure?

1. Do you mix business with pleasure?
2. Do you take your business interactions personally?
3. Have you ever made a heart decision when you should have made a head one?
4. Do our business "issues" reflect us as everything else in our lives does?
5. Have you ever explored your business issues based on how they make you feel?

Group-Specific

Community Building Conversation Starters

Note: These will likely take longer than one meeting unless that one meeting is several hours long.

Community Building with a Church Group

1. Introduce yourself using three words that best describe you.
2. What is your earliest memory of church?
3. Did you grow up in this faith or did you enter the faith later?
4. What was the first church you went to and how old were you?
5. What did you like about the church service? What do you like most about it now?
6. What did you not like about the church service?
7. What does your church-going give you?
8. What do you most want for the children of this congregation?
9. What do you want most for the teenagers and youth?
10. What do you feel is the most important aspect of a relationship to your faith?
11. Do you feel the church caters enough to the needs of the congregation?
12. What do you feel is the church's relationship to the city/town and what do you wish it would be?
13. Finish this sentence, "The thing I want most for this group of people who gather to worship is…"
14. Finish this sentence, "The thing I want most for myself in a church community is…"

Community Building in the PTA

1. Introduce yourself sharing how many children you have and what grades they are in school.

2. Continue that introduction of yourself sharing your chosen career and marital status.
3. Tell us who you are using just three words which have nothing to do with your children, career or marital status.
4. Share what brought you to this meeting - what drew you to become involved?
5. What was your experience of school growing up - i.e. where did you go to school, what was it like, did you enjoy school?
6. What do you feel are the best parts of the schools you attended? Do you see any of these elements in this school?
7. What is your highest hope/vision for the children of this school?
8. What is this school not doing well enough that it can do better?
9. What are the greatest strengths of this school?
10. What most recommends you to this committee? For instance; passion, interest, experience, concern, willingness to get to work?
11. What do you feel are the most important issues that we should address?
12. How do you see the connection between the school, the parents, and the PTA? How can we strengthen those connections?

Community Building with Family Daycare Owners

1. Why did you want to open a daycare?
2. What two challenges were the toughest to overcome in doing this?
3. What worked best for you to fill your spots?
4. What has proven to be your best idea for the daycare so far?
5. What is your greatest gift as an educator?
6. What's one skill you wish you had?
7. Finish this sentence, "It's been a good day if…"
8. Finish this sentence, "It's been a beautiful day if…"
9. If you had unlimited funds, what would you change about your daycare?
10. What is the biggest personal challenge you face in running your daycare?

11. Finish this sentence, "My favourite activity with the kids is..."
12. What was your greatest fear in opening and operating a daycare?
13. What books have influenced you and shaped you as an educator?
14. What one person influenced you on your journey to open a daycare?
15. What teacher influenced you the most and why?
16. What three values do you strive to instill in your children?
17. What is your future vision for your daycare?
18. How has your experience working with children impacted your personally?
19. Finish this sentence, "When I started this business I never imagined I could..."
20. Finish this sentence, "After my children graduate, I want them to fondly remember me for..."
21. Finish this sentence, "My best characteristic as an educator is my..."
22. Finish this sentence, "I am so happy I opened a daycare because..."

Community Building in a Neighbourhood

1. What is the first neighbourhood you can remember - what do you remember about it?
2. How did you feel as you played in that neighbourhood?
3. Were there any remarkable characters in your neighbourhood?
4. How did the children interact?
5. Did the mothers socialize? How? Did the fathers? Did they socialize as couples?
6. Did you ever go Christmas Carolling around the neighbourhood?
7. Did the neighbours support one another in that first neighbourhood and in others where you've lived? How?
8. Did you feel the neighbours were looking out for your children as you looked out for theirs?
9. Tell us about the most memorable neighbour you've had.
10. Share your fondest neighbourhood memory.

Community Building with City Council Members and Staff

1. How long have you been on a city council or working for it?
2. What prompted you to run for city council or to apply for a job here?
3. What do you see as the three best qualities of this city?
4. Do you find it difficult to do all the things you want to do?
5. What do you see as the three top issues that need to be addressed?
6. What is your biggest frustration with the running of the city?
7. What is your greatest praise for this collaborative group?
8. What else could we do to make this city a beautiful place to live?

Community Building with a Mom's Group

1. How old were you when you had your first child?
2. How many children do you have or do you want to have?
3. What was the most surprising thing about having a baby in your care?
4. Who is your mentor as a mom?
5. Did you have support for the first few days when you brought your baby home? Do you still have support?
6. What is your favourite parenting routine?
7. What are your goals as a parent? (i.e. I want to instil confidence in my children, give them unconditional love, etc.)
8. What do you want your child/children to have that you did not have growing up?
9. How do you (plan to) handle technology and the allure of screen time and games with your children?
10. What lullabies do you sing to your children?
11. What was your greatest fear as a new mom?
12. How do you mitigate your fears?
13. What books do you read to your children?
14. What are your fondest dreams and hopes for your children?
15. What did you wish you knew before you became a mom?

Other Sources of Conversation Starters

No matter why we come together to build community; a project, a topic, cause or even the desire to have a community building experience, the first thing we do is get to know one another on a deeper level. My blog, *Lifeforinstance.com*, is a resource of many life-theme questions that can be used to spark a discussion. Choose from the archives any topic that speaks to you. Begin by reading the short post and then use the questions at the end of the post as a stimulus for discussion. Before the meeting, prepare more questions to go with it, or announce the post/topic and ask each person bring a question to the meeting.

Alternately, use your favourite search engine to search for more Life themed blogs and find topics there.

Community Building Games

These are games that serve as community building exercises for the group that is working its way to community. Save them until you've met as a group for a significant number of hours and are well acquainted. If your group is in pseudocommunity or even chaos, these exercises will contribute to your community building efforts. If the group is already in community, they will help to deepen your connections and increase your camaraderie.

The Community Name Game

This is a fun game to play with your group. It came up in a discussion on a Hangout one day. I was listening to Corinne talking and she said, *"A high tide raises all boats."* I suddenly remembered a game we had played with our children and realized it was a game we could play as a group. *"I know what your Community Name is,"* I said, *"You are "High Tide"*. Yes, Corinne is the one in the group who raises the spirits of the others. Stu immediately laughed in agreement with me. Then I explained the inspiration behind what we came to call the Community Name Game.

Years ago, when our children were small, we went on a clam digging, camping weekend with friends. As we walked along the mud flats searching for clams, our friend told a story to the children, then aged three and five. Many years ago, North American Indians used to walk these flats looking for their food, she said. At that point, she turned to our daughter who looked a little like Pocahontas with her poker-straight black hair. "You are *Black Raven*," she said, giving her a special name. Our three-year-old son was hopping around looking for the holes, which indicated the presence of clams. She dubbed him *Searching Panther*. The game extended to the adults who slowly received their camping names. One by one, as we went about our activities that weekend, the names for one another were revealed.

The names came organically, based on our observations of one another. They were all positive in nature and no one was allowed to name him or herself. My Husband was *He Who Finds a Better Way*, a perfect name as anyone who knows him would attest. I was called *She Who Waits With Patience*. By the end of our camping trip, everyone had received a name. Finding and assigning names became a tradition we carried on with anyone who joined us on camping trips. Though over twenty years have passed since that camping trip, we all still remember our names.

The Community Name Game is a good game to play with a group of people who are building community. It calls on us to pay attention to one another, it unifies the group and it's fun.

Note: we have to be aware that our names can change as we grow and evolve. Changing someone's name can be an indication of their growth as observed and affirmed by the members of their community. This is all part of the fun.

Name the Team

A variation on the Community Name Game is Name the Team. In this game, the group is challenged to find a name for the group. Suggestions for this name could come about organically as you go about the meeting activities, or you could play consensus to come up with a name. It should be a name that seems logical and obvious to the members of the group. Also, like the Community Name Game, Name the Team is a group-unifying exercise and your name can change over time.

Assigning a name to your family, for instance, creates a unifying group identity. Yes, my husband, daughter, son and I are a family but when we identify with the name "Team Gosselin", there is an additional layer of awareness of our identity, our special connection and our importance to one another.

The Gift Game

In this game, the members confer "gifts" on one another. You can use the following topics (select one per game) or add some of your own.

1. If I could, I would give you an all-expense paid, luxury trip to _____.
2. I would love to give you a complete renovation of one room in your home - the _____ room.

3. If I could give you an all-paid shopping trip it would be
   to_____.
4. If I could give you something you would love to have but
   wouldn't buy for yourself, I would give you...
5. I'd love to wave a magic wand and give you ten free days in
   this summer place_____
6. I'd like to give you a course you'd enjoy, enrolment in a
   _____ class.
7. If I could give you one superhero power, it would be

   _____.

8. I imagine a perfect day for you would include these three
   things _____.

The Truth Game

When we meet friends or acquaintances, the standard greeting is
"How are you?" and the typical response is, *"Fine. How are you?"*
In this game, we learn to give the truthful, authentic answer,
something members of a community do.

Take turns answering the question, "How are you?" Think of the
question as *"How have you been? What's been happening in your
life? What's been on your mind? What exciting things are in your
life these days? What concerns are you nursing?"* One by one,
answer the question. As each person answers, the others listen
carefully. They can respond in validation and empathy with the
person speaking.

Let me share an example. On the day I am writing this, if I played
this game, this would be my answer.

> *"I'm feeling tired. This week I picked up my new computer
> that I researched and purchased myself. It made me miss
> Alex, who would have advised me on this purchase, as he
> knew so much about computers. On the day I shut down the
> old computer for the last time, the computer he had set up for
> us in this room, I felt overwhelmed with sadness. All week I'd*

been heart-thumping tired and not able to sleep well. On the day before and on the day I picked up the computer, I had shooting pain on the left side of my face, in my jaw and cheekbones. Finally, I realized what it was about; letting go of one more part of Alex, the computer where we worked together, which connected us. When I cried about it, the pain dissipated. I guess I'm still a bit tired from the emotional release."

Community is about authentically connecting with our fellow human beings. Once the group has achieved community, you won't need this game because the members will be interacting this way all the time. But it is a good idea to play it now and then anyway, to remind everyone that your connections as members of a community go far beneath the surface.

The Double-Dare Game

A variation of the Truth Game is to have each person share something of truth, something they may need to express. The things that hurt us most in life, causing health problems and stress, are emotions we deny. This really amounts to not being honest with oneself. Honesty and integrity are hallmarks of community. In a community, one can express things they may not feel comfortable expressing elsewhere.

You may find that the first time you play the game, the truths expressed are not deep, but give it time. It's like a muscle you tone. After a while, like the truth game, it will feel more natural to share easily within your community.

The "What I Like About You" Game

Everyone wants to feel special, perhaps because it's the truest state of our being, but few of us emerge from childhood with "specialness" as part of our personal identity. This game shows us how other people see us, something we rarely glimpse. Here's how the game works in an offline setting and in an online one.

OFFLINE: Everyone is given a pen and a stack of small pieces of paper. Each person writes down something special about each person in the room, making a separate note for each person present. They fold the notes and put them all in a hat. When everyone has finished, one person at a time draws a piece of paper from the hat and reads what's been written and the others guess who is the subject of the special note. The subject of each Special paper is given the paper to keep.

ONLINE: Everyone writes down the names of everyone else in the group and next to each name writes down something special about each person. One by one each person randomly selects a note and reads it to the group who then try to guess who it is about. Each person can, if they like, make note of what the others have said about them.

The "Who Knew?" Game

Each person shares something that nobody knows about them and then asks for a show of hands, "Who knew this?" This game, like many of the others, is best played after the members have spent a significant amount of time together.

Bring a Joke to Dinner Game

Family dinners are great opportunities for community building. Here is a game to play during the meal or while enjoying dessert and tea.

Let everyone know in advance that they need to bring one joke to the table. It has to be clean and wholesome and appropriate for all ages. At some point in the meal, one by one begin to share your jokes.

Your group may discover more community building games. Community building is about connecting through authentic communication and enjoying the incredible camaraderie that results. What could be more fun than that?

Gratitude

I want to wholeheartedly express my gratitude to…

- The Hangout Group: None of this would have happened without you Corinne, Veronica, Don, Stu, Rose and Jim. (Pseudonyms - but you know who you are!)
- Auguste Gosselin, hand model, for his photography input and support.
- Emily Dickinson for her early read and feedback, Joe Huxtable, who read two versions of the manuscript.
- Beke, web designer extraordinaire, for the logo and the author site Wordpress theme and the help in putting it all together.
- Julie, my sister, for taking the photos for the author site and for the book's cover photo and design, and of course for reading the manuscript and providing feedback.
- My nieces, Jessica and Melanie, who helped me to flesh out the subject as I began to develop it. Thanks, Jess for reading it so many times over those three years!
- Tony Abbass, my father, who read it very quickly early on and my brother, Allan Abbass, who gave it a once-over and a thumbs up at the very end!
- Steve Rice, Barbara Klein and Claudia Scimeca, who provided such great feedback.
- MicheleAust, my editor, who polished and cleaned up the manuscript when I finally surrendered it into her hands.
- Natasha Gosselin, my daughter, for her professional--and personal--feedback. And for asking the second question that inspired the writing of a book. I don't dare wonder what question she will she ask next.

RESOURCES

THE DIFFERENT DRUM; Community Making and Peace
By M. Scott Peck, M.D.
Simon & Schuster, New York, New York
Copyright 1987

MEMOIRS
Pierre Elliott Trudeau,
McClelland & Stewart Inc. Toronto Ontario,
Copyright 1993

BELONGING: The Paradox of Citizenship
By Adrienne Clarkson
House of Anansi Press Inc. Toronto, Ontario
Copyright 2014

HARDWIRING HAPPINESS: The New Brain Science of Contentment,
Calm, and Confidence
By Rick Hanson, Ph.D.
Harmony Publishers, an imprint of the Crown Publishing Group, a division
of Random House LLC, a Penguin Random House Company, New York
Copyright 2013

THE INNOVATORS: How a Group of Hackers, Geniuses, and
Geeks Created the Digital Revolution
By Walter Isaacson
Simon & Schuster, New York, New York
Copyright 2014

ROOTS OF EMPATHY: Changing the World Child by Child
By Mary Gordon
Thomas Allen Publishers, Toronto, Ontario
Copyright 2005

LONELINESS; Human Nature and the Need for Social Connection
John T. Cacioppo and William Patrick
W.W. Norton & Company, New York, London
Copyright 2008

WHY AM I AFRAID TO TELL YOU WHO I AM? Insights into Personal Growth
By John Powell
Thomas More; Pf edition
Copyright 1969

BOWLING ALONE: The Collapse and Revival of American Community
By Robert D. Putnam
Simon & Schuster Paperbacks. New York, New York
Copyright 2000

MIND OVER MEDICINE: Scientific Proof That You Can Heal Yourself
By Lissa Rankin
Hay House, Inc.
Copyright 2013

REACHING THROUGH RESISTANCE: Advanced Psychotherapy Techniques
By Allan Abbass, MD
Seven Leaves Press, Kansas City, MO
Copyright 2015

SPONTANEOUS EVOLUTION: Our Positive Future and a Way to Get There From Here
By Bruce H. Lipton, Ph.D. and Steve Bhaerman
Mountain of Love Productions and Steve Bhaerman
Copyright 2009

DEEPENING COMMUNITY; Finding Joy Together in Chaotic Times
By Paul Born
Berrett-Koehler Publishers Inc, San Francisco, CA
Copyright 2014

HOLD ON TO YOUR KIDS: Why Parents Need to Matter More Than Peers
By Gordon Neufeld, PhD and Gabor Mate, MD
Copyright 2004, Postscript copyright 2013
Vintage Canada Edition, 2013

KIDS ARE WORTH IT!: Giving Your Child The Gift Of Inner Discipline
By Barbara Coloroso
HarperCollins Publishers Inc., New York, NY
Copyright 1994

THE WHOLE-BRAIN CHILD: 12 Revolutionary strategies to nurture your child's developing mind.
by Daniel J. Siegel, M.D. and Tina Payne Bryson, PhD.
Bantam Books Trade Paperback edition
Copyright 2011 by Mind Your Brain, Inc., and Bryson Creative Productions, Inc.

THE EXPLOSIVE CHILD: A New Approach for Understanding and Parenting Easily Frustrated, Chronically Inflexible Children
By Ross W. Greene PhD
Harper Collins Publisher, New York, New York
Copyright 1998

FREE TO LEARN: Why Unleashing the Instinct to Play Will Make Our Children, Happier, More Self-Reliant, and Better Students for Life
By Peter Gray
Basic Books
Copyright 2013

POCKET NEIGHBORHOODS; Creating Small-scale Community in a Large-scale World
By Ross Chapin
The Taunton Press Inc., Newton CT
Copyright 2011

LEADERS EAT LAST; Why Some Teams Pull Together and Others Don't
By Simon Sinek
The Penguin Group, New York, New York
Copyright 2014

ABOUT THE AUTHOR

Lori Gosselin believes the power of community transforms lives. At her blog, *Life, for Instance*, she delivers the core message of community: *We are all in this together.*

Her first book, *The Happy Place*, introduces a profound system for healing emotional wounds.

Connect with her at http://www.lorigosselin.com to join the discussion.

.

www.ingramcontent.com/pod-product-compliance
Lightning Source LLC
Chambersburg PA
CBHW050131280326
41933CB00010B/1326